RUNNING AGAINST THE HERD

RUNNING AGAINST THE HERD

Battling Biases to Make Better Investment Decisions

EDDIE PERKIN

Columbia Business School
Publishing

Columbia University Press
Publishers Since 1893
New York Chichester, West Sussex
cup.columbia.edu

Library of Congress Cataloging-in-Publication Data

Names: Perkin, Eddie author.
Title: Running against the herd : battling biases to make better investment decisions / Eddie Perkin.
Description: New York : Columbia University Press, [2026] |
Includes bibliographical references and index
Identifiers: LCCN 2026004714 | ISBN 9780231224147 hardback |
ISBN 9780231565523 ebook | ISBN 9780231567718 PDF
Subjects: LCSH: Investments—Psychological aspects. |
Investments—Decision making.
Classification: LCC HG4515.15 .P47 2026
LC record available at https://lccn.loc.gov/2026004714

Cover design: Noah Arlow
Cover images: Shutterstock

GPSR Authorized Representative: Easy Access System Europe,
Mustamäe tee 50, 10621 Tallinn, Estonia, gpsr.requests@easproject.com

To my children, Alex, James, and Natalia,
three masters of constructive conflict.

CONTENTS

RUNNING AGAINST THE HERD

INTRODUCTION

Abraham Lincoln, when facing the decision of whether to issue the Emancipation Proclamation, polled the members of his cabinet. Each saw only downsides and voted against the idea. The president reflected for a moment, leaned back in his chair, and said, "Well gentlemen, that makes seven 'nays' and only one 'aye.' The ayes have it."

THE APOCRYPHAL STORY of Abraham Lincoln's decisiveness in the face of opposition cleverly illustrates the boldness and vision sometimes required of a leader. Committees come up short when the desire for consensus and conflict avoidance lead to caution and groupthink.[1]

The goal of this book is to demonstrate how a team of individuals with diverse perspectives and areas of expertise can overcome groupthink and their own cognitive biases to make better decisions. The lessons and examples are drawn largely from the world of professional investing, but they have universal applications.

Although all investors aspire to "buy low and sell high," many end up doing the opposite. The effect is so strong that retail investors achieved an average annual return over ten years that was 1.2 percent per year less than the overall return of the mutual funds and exchange-traded funds (ETFs) in which they were invested.[2]

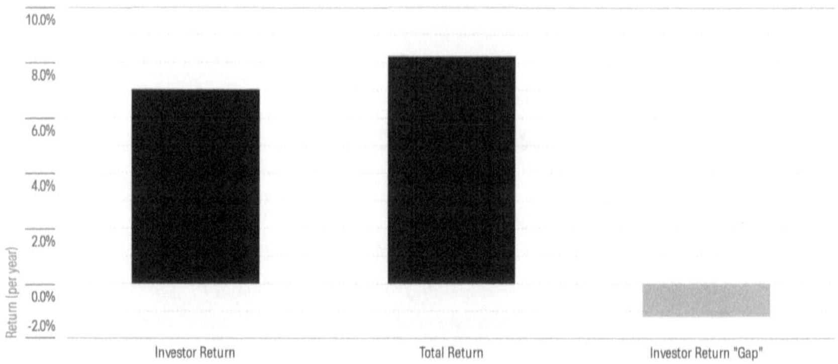

FIGURE 0.1 Annual investor returns and total returns of US open-ended funds and ETFs (10 years ended December 31, 2024).

Source: Morningstar, author's calculations. Data as of December 31, 2024. Excludes "commodities" category groups and funds of funds.

Even professional investors who tend to be good at identifying stocks to buy, on average, do a poor job of deciding when to sell. In my observation, this poor "sell discipline" is directly connected to several cognitive biases that are commonplace throughout the asset management industry.

My own experience is different. The independent firm Cabot Research studied every trade made over three years for the European equity fund, which I managed while at Goldman

Sachs, and reported that they rarely came across a portfolio where such a high percentage of the outperformance came from knowing when to sell. I am convinced that the big difference in the quality of sell decisions versus competitors is a function of the ideas discussed in this book.

Until early 2023, I was the chief investment officer (CIO), Equity, at Eaton Vance (a subsidiary of Morgan Stanley), where I led a department of seventy professionals based in three countries with responsibility for $75 billion of client assets invested in global stocks. Prior to that, I was the CIO for International and Emerging Markets Equity at Goldman Sachs Asset Management.

This book's ideas and solutions were refined over more than two decades working in leadership roles in asset management. The teams that I have led, and the portfolios that I have managed personally, have beaten the relevant stock market benchmarks, including the S&P 500, Russell 2000, Russell 1000 Value, MSCI EAFE, and MSCI World. Results were robust across regions, styles, sectors, and market capitalization ranges.

When I left Goldman Sachs Asset Management, each of the eight developed markets equity funds that I oversaw had three-year investment performance that had beaten their respective benchmarks. At the time of my departure from Eaton Vance, ten of fourteen equity funds that I oversaw had ten-year track records ahead of their respective benchmarks.[3]

Over the years, when I spoke with prospective clients and consultants about our investment process and how we were different from our competitors, I would describe many of the ideas in this book and offer examples like the Robinson Crusoe portfolio exercise (described in chapter 10, on short-termism).

This practical example of how we reoriented our thinking to the long-term prospects of our companies resonated, and one of the large investment consulting firms told me that they had never seen an equity team be so purposeful and deliberate about addressing groupthink and cognitive bias in their investment process. Another consultant told a colleague, "Someone should write a book on this stuff."

I believe that a well-organized team operating with an ethos of productive conflict and employing the tools described throughout this book can excel as a highly effective decision-making unit.

Professional investors are likely to benefit the most from this book and the prescriptive solutions that it offers. Real-life examples drawn from the world of $100 million-plus investment decisions will resonate. Capital allocators, investment consultants, and trustees should appreciate the content on incentives and sell discipline. Individual investors who aspire to beat the pros will also find actionable ideas.

Adjacent to this target audience is the reader who works with others in any small to mid-sized group. This could be a committee, board of directors, school study group, task force, team, or other type of working unit. Whether your role in the group is that of leader, junior member, or something in between, you will be able to make immediate use of the ideas in this book. Most of these solutions come from my experience leading investment teams, but the concepts can easily be repurposed for other domains.

In March 1979, Amos Tversky and Daniel Kahneman published their seminal academic paper "Prospect Theory: An

Analysis of Decision Under Risk," helping to launch the school of behavioral economics.[4] It challenged the accepted wisdom in classical economics that human beings are utility-maximizing rational actors, logically weighing each of the pros and cons of a decision in real time, with an emotionally detached mind. In the years since, countless studies have been undertaken, deepening the understanding of human fallibility and bias. Estimates on the total number of cognitive biases sum to more than 180.[5] In recent years, the Nobel Prize in Economic Sciences has been awarded to at least six individuals who could be considered behavioral economists, including Kahneman himself in 2002.[6]

And yet tangible solutions to these well-documented sources of poor decision making have largely been lacking. *Running Against the Herd* aims to address that void.

Typically, we are told to "be aware of our biases," and it ends at that. But what about those of us who want to improve our decision making by going into combat against the shortcomings of our mental shortcuts, heuristics, rules of thumb, instincts, and other baggage that we carry in our heads? Can we perhaps even flip these biases around to work in our favor and turn vice into virtue? If you are someone who acknowledges your own human infallibility and you want to take action to address it, keep reading.

This book is separated into two parts.

Part I goes into depth on the fifteen cognitive biases that I believe have the strongest negative influence on investment decisions. Each chapter focuses on a single bias, beginning with an example, touching briefly on the scholarly research that was conducted to identify the bias, and proposing tools and techniques that my former colleagues and I used to overcome it. Each chapter ends with a summary list of three solutions, which are fleshed out in further detail in the appendix. These chapters need not be read in a specific order, so you can feel free to hop in and out of the material as you see fit.

Each chapter begins with two epigraphs, quotations from famous individuals past and present. These wise and motivational one-liners connect to the subject matter of the chapter. They also frequently contradict one another. I see this as neatly illustrating the yin and yang of cognitive biases. Mental shortcuts serve us well most of the time, but it also pays to occasionally stop and think deeply when a decision is complex or consequential.[7] After all, the ancient Greek philosophers advised, "everything in moderation." Then again, actress Mae West observed, "Too much of a good thing can be wonderful."

Part II is for current and prospective leaders. It discusses how to build and lead teams to take the lessons from part I, overcome groupthink, and become a world-class decision-making unit. Team size, culture, process, and incentives are all parts of the success formula. As in part I, each chapter offers three solutions that are also summarized in the appendix.

I have come to believe that acting as a fiduciary, professionally investing on behalf of others, is one of the most rewarding and challenging careers that one can pursue. In this line of work, you are competing against many highly intelligent, well-educated, abundantly resourced people and their machines. The job has a balance between collaborating with others on an investment team in pursuit of a common goal and the individual accountability that comes with being personally responsible for investment decisions. To be successful, you need the right mix of confidence and humility.

As legendary hedge fund manager Seth Klarman has said, it takes a level of arrogance to think that one can win in such a game:

> In investing, whenever you act, you are effectively saying, I know more than the market. I am going to buy when everybody else is selling. I am going to sell when everybody else is buying. That is arrogant, and we always need to temper it with the humility of knowing we could be wrong—that things can change—and acknowledging that we have a lot of smart competitors.[8]

Many academic economists take this insight to the extreme and argue that the market cannot be beaten. The efficient market hypothesis (EMH) claims that all relevant information is fully reflected in stock prices, making it impossible to do better than average on a sustained basis.[9]

Regulation Fair Disclosure (Reg FD), implemented by the US Securities and Exchange Commission (SEC) in October 2000, attempted to ensure that the proverbial little guy was not informationally disadvantaged by virtue of public company executives disclosing material, nonpublic information to a select group of favored investors. Rather than pivoting to a new approach, many professional investors continue to treat investing as a game of information gathering. He who has the most data wins the game. This has led to the heavy use of expert professional networks and artificial intelligence.[10]

The path less trodden is to wave the white flag on efforts to gain an informational advantage. Instead, focus on making better decisions with the data that one already has. This approach starts with first confessing one's own shortcomings. We are all biased.[11] Once that admission has been made, liberation follows. The next step is to use tools and processes tailored to overcome specific biases.

Finally, a word about the book's title. Images of bulls are common on Wall Street. Merrill Lynch's 13,000 financial advisors have been called the "thundering herd." But to outperform the market, one must do something different.

I challenge you to embrace the mindset of the independent thinker and join me in running against the herd.

PART I

Fifteen Biases and Their Solutions

Chapter One

THE ENDOWMENT EFFECT

Don't ever give up!
—Jimmy Valvano, former North Carolina State basketball coach, ESPY Awards (1993)

The grass is always greener on the other side.
—Ovid, *Metamorphoses*

SCOTT WAS in the market for a new car. He had just turned forty and was newly single. He had done some preliminary research online and spoken extensively with a couple of friends to get their advice. He had narrowed his options to three vehicles and was now ready to visit three dealers. He walked onto the lot of the first, a BMW dealership. An attractive young salesperson named Lisa quickly found him and showed him the inventory. He liked the look of the M3 in Interlagos blue.

"Scott, let me open the door for you. Climb inside and see how it feels."

He sank into the stitched leather driver's seat and wrapped his fingers around the steering wheel. Indeed, he liked how it felt. The next helpful suggestion from Lisa was taking a test drive. Once they were on the open road, she asked Scott about his favorite type of music.

"I like '80s rock," came the quick reply.

Lisa started the vehicle's satellite radio, found a classic rock station, and turned up the volume as Van Halen's "Panama" pumped from the speakers.

"Give it some gas, Scott." He obliged.

As they turned back into the dealer lot after the short test drive, Lisa whispered, "Scott, I can really see you in this car. It's you."

Lisa was not the only one who could see Scott in the car. He could see himself in it. In fact, during that short drive, his imagination had gotten the better of him. There he was picking up a date in his shiny new M3. He could almost hear his friends whistling in admiration as they saw him drive up for the first time. This was *his* car.

When Lisa informed Scott that this was the only M3 in stock and she had an appointment with another potential buyer at the top of the hour, Scott's mind was made up. He was not going to allow someone else to take *his* car. The paperwork was quickly completed, and thoughts of the other two vehicles that he had been considering evaporated.

What Scott experienced was a case of the endowment effect.[1] With the encouragement of a clever salesperson, he allowed himself to feel that he already possessed the car, which left him with the perception that it was more valuable to him than alternatives. He abandoned the clear-headed research process that he had undertaken to make this important, expensive decision, and he allowed his emotions to get the better of him.

Of the dozens of cognitive biases that have been identified, I believe that none is more pernicious for investors than the endowment effect and its close cousin, loss aversion.[2]

Examples of the endowment effect are all around us. Companies and salespeople use the endowment effect to their advantage.

In addition to automobile test drives, examples include thirty-day trials, free returns, and trying on clothing. Each of these supposed freebies is designed to encourage a sense of emotional attachment and a feeling of ownership and possession.

The term "endowment effect" was coined in 1980 by Richard Thaler. He later collaborated with Daniel Kahneman and Jack Knetsch to conduct research on the topic.[3] The experiment consisted of giving a coffee mug to everyone in a group of students. A market was then established to allow the mugs to be traded for something of equal value. Classical economic theory suggests that half the mugs should have been exchanged and half retained. In practice, though, the students who had been endowed with a mug showed a preference for retaining it, and few mugs were exchanged.

The endowment effect occurs when individuals place greater value on something that they own than what they would be willing to pay to acquire the same object if they did not own it. It is suggested that the endowment effect results from *loss aversion*, which is the tendency for humans to find the level of pain from losses to be stronger than the level of pleasure from equivalent-sized gains. Giving up something that one owns feels like a loss, whereas not acquiring it in the first place does not.

It is not difficult to see the endowment effect's role in investing decisions. Clichés like "riding your losers down" speak directly to the damage that it can cause. It is the bane of the value investor, someone who looks to buy what is cheap and sell what is dear. It is almost a mark of pride for the value investor to say the equivalent of, "If I liked it at 100, I love it at 80." Mathematically, this is true if nothing new has been learned in the interim about the fundamental merits of the investment. However, the price of an asset does not fall from 100 to 80 without a reason. A rational, cool-headed evaluation of whether the 20 percent drop is warranted by the facts is what is called for, not a reflexive statement of bravado that liberates investors from confronting the possibility that they might have gotten it wrong.

Professional sports bettors understand this concept of listening to the market. If a betting line in which they are interested does not get repriced after they make a large bet, they become concerned. This resistance from the market tells them that there might be smart money on the other side of the bet. This was illustrated for me during a conversation I had over lunch with a sharp bettor who specializes in forecasting run totals for Major League Baseball (MLB). His process is to run his sophisticated prediction model the day before games and, if there are any mispriced lines when the betting markets open later that evening, place his bets that very night rather than waiting for game day. Toward the end of our discussion, I asked him if there were any bets he liked in that afternoon's games. "Well, all the lines I liked last night have moved except for the total in the Padres game. But I wouldn't bet that one now. Since the line hasn't moved, I'm probably wrong, and it's not a good bet anymore." I was struck by the humility of that statement and realized that this was a guy who respects the market and is willing to let go of his favored ideas.

In the world of professional team sports, particularly the National Football League (NFL), the endowment effect can negatively influence personnel decisions. Veteran players, particularly those who are fan favorites, will often be re-signed to expensive contracts just as their individual performance begins to deteriorate. One team that seemingly found a way to buck this trend over two decades was the New England Patriots. Owner Bob Kraft and head coach Bill Belichick demonstrated a willingness to absorb the ire of fans by letting go of stars like Ty Law, Adam Vinatieri, Richard Seymour, Mike Vrabel, and Chandler Jones. Even Tom Brady was eventually allowed to leave, showing that there were no sacred cows.

There are several tools that I have employed to combat the endowment effect within myself and our investment teams. Periodically, I would ask each member of the team to take a blank sheet of paper and perform a zero-based rebuild of the portfolio. Each person was expected to work independently to construct the portfolio anew, without referring to what was currently owned. I instructed the team to imagine that we have a brand-new client, funding its account with us for the first time. With no legacy positions or mental baggage, what portfolio would we build for this new client? Assuming that the old and new clients have the same risk tolerance, time horizon, and guideline restrictions, if this new portfolio is meaningfully different from the current one, why would we not immediately make trades to move to the ideal? The only acceptable answers that I have found are transaction costs and tax considerations.

This portfolio exercise should be performed by multiple parties. Each of these colleagues can perform the function of what professional poker player Annie Duke calls a "quitting coach."[4] These colleagues are close enough to the decision to understand the context, but distant enough not to experience the endowment effect directly themselves. They also understand that it is their duty to disagree and speak up.

It is also important that the starting point is literally blank. Do not simply take a list of current portfolio holdings and mark it up. Each position must be justified anew. Replacement holdings are encouraged, even if the ideas are only half-baked. As with zero-based budgeting, the starting point should be zero or one risks falling victim to the inertia and baseline of what is already in place, a form of anchoring bias.

At Eaton Vance, we had tax-specialist portfolio managers who would talk about "keeping the quarter." The "quarter" was the roughly 25 percent that would otherwise be paid to Uncle Sam in capital gains taxes. In practice, keeping the quarter meant letting winners run (and grow tax deferred) and cutting losers short (to crystallize valuable tax deductions). I found this cultural legacy of viewing a "harvestable" tax loss as something to be utilized helpful in countering the potential damage of the endowment effect. In a sense, it turns the endowment effect on its head by mentally acknowledging an asset that one can monetize only by letting the loser go.

Under this mindset, disposing of a portfolio holding that is in a loss position is no longer something about which to be embarrassed, but rather a value-creation opportunity to be undertaken on behalf of clients. After the thirty-day wash sale period clears, one may elect to repurchase the shares, but by then it is truly a fresh decision, and any false loyalty that one feels toward the stock will have dissipated.

In my own experience with running a tax-managed value equity portfolio alongside a similar one without the tax constraint, the tax-managed version performed modestly better. Despite slightly higher fees, the ten-year outperformance of the tax-managed strategy has been roughly 25 basis points (0.25 percent) better on a *pretax basis* despite—or because of—the extra constraint.

While tax-conscious investors can use the wash-sale rule to enforce a cooling-off period, tax-free investors, as well as decision makers in other settings, should look for opportunities to create similar circuit breakers for themselves. The idea is to turn the decision into a fresh one rather than defaulting to the status quo.

The endowment effect need not be solely about holding onto a losing position. Falling in love with a stock or other cherished asset that has treated you well can lead to lost perspective and overlooked opportunities of greater value.

SOLUTION SUMMARY

1. **Perform a zero-based rebuild.** Start with the assumption that you do not possess the thing in question. Do you want it now? For the purposes of this exercise, assume no frictional costs in getting to the new, ideal state.
2. **Find a quitting coach.** A quitting coach is a form of devil's advocate but is more specifically someone who understands that his or her role is to help you avoid large investments of money, time, or effort in something that is unlikely to pay off. As Duke would advise, this person must be willing to tell you what you may not want to hear, and you must be willing to listen.
3. **Respect the market.** When the collective wisdom of the crowd continues to tell you over a period of time that you are wrong, listen to it, and search for reasons that you might have things wrong.

Chapter Two

SUNK-COST FALLACY

If at first you don't succeed, try, try again.
—Edward Hickson, British writer, 1857

It's no use crying over spilled milk.
—James Howell, British historian, 1659

A JOKE that I once heard vividly—and literally—illustrates the concept of sunk cost:

> A man tells a friend that earlier that day, he had accidentally dropped a one-dollar bill into a port-a-potty toilet. "So I took out a hundred-dollar bill and threw that one in also." The friend frowned and asked, "Why on earth would you do that?" His answer: "If you think I am going to go fishing around in all that muck for a measly dollar, you are crazy! I had to make it worth my while."

Sunk costs are those that have already been borne where there is no way to reclaim them or receive a refund.[1] The costs may be monetary, emotional, or even temporal. The key insight from economics is that sunk costs should have no bearing on the decision to spend further resources or effort on the endeavor. The cost is sunk—gone forever.

And yet people have trouble embracing the mindset of letting go. Here are a few examples:

- The CEO of a public company makes an expensive acquisition of a smaller company in an adjacent business line. After three years, the new division is losing money, and there is no hope for a turnaround. Not wanting to admit defeat, the CEO continues to invest in the business despite the red ink.
- Weeks ago, you bought tickets to an NFL game. The day of the game has arrived. Your friend can no longer attend the game with you, the temperature is much colder than expected (and snowy to boot), and the team finds itself in last place, with the star quarterback injured. If the tickets had been free or received as a gift, you would no longer bother to go. However, since you "spent good money," you trudge out to the game and have a miserable time.
- You are dining out at a buffet. The food is not very tasty, and you already feel full, but you go back for a second helping to "get your money's worth."

The recognition of the fallacy of sunk costs is illustrated by how many clichés have been developed to describe the mentality that one should have:

- It's no use crying over spilled milk.
- It's water under the bridge.
- It's water over the dam.
- That ship has sailed.
- Don't bother closing the barn door after the horse has bolted.

- You can't put toothpaste back in the tube.
- The genie is out of the bottle.
- The cake is already baked.
- Let bygones be bygones.
- Don't throw good money after bad.
- We've crossed the Rubicon.
- We've gone beyond the point of no return.
- Let it go.
- It's too late now.
- We're on to Cincinnati.
- Be a goldfish.

Economist Richard Thaler defined sunk costs as follows:

> Economic theory implies that only incremental costs and benefits *should* affect decisions. Historical costs should be irrelevant. But do (non-economist) consumers ignore sunk costs in their everyday decisions? . . . I do not believe that they do. Rather, I suggest the alternative hypothesis that paying for the right to use a good or service will increase the rate at which the good will be utilized, ceteris paribus. This hypothesis will be referred to as the *sunk cost effect*.[2]

I am convinced that one source of the psychological blind spot that prevents many of us from thinking about sunk costs as economically rational actors comes from our parents and grandparents. From childhood, many of us were taught to "clean your plate" and "waste not, want not." Wrapped up in the psychological baggage of sunk costs are the admirable qualities of thriftiness and frugality.

In investing, sunk costs can take both monetary and nonmonetary forms. Money tied up in an investment that has gone south is unavailable for an alternative, possibly better idea, which has the effect of turning sunk costs into opportunity costs.

The nonmonetary form of sunk costs can also be damaging. Consider a professional equity analyst who has spent several weeks, or even months, developing an investment idea. They have flown out to visit the company headquarters to interview senior management and inspect the operations. They have conducted channel checks and site visits to interview the company's customers, vendors, and competitors. An elaborate, multitabbed Microsoft Excel model has been built, with detailed financial forecasts and valuation work. The investment case has been presented to colleagues, and the stock has been bought by several of the firm's portfolio managers who followed the analyst's recommendation. This individual is not only financially but emotionally invested in the outcome, and they have spent a lot of time and energy getting to this point. In the future, if new risks emerge or the investment merits deteriorate, the analyst may feel reluctant to move on to something new, given the time and effort that they have already put in. But that time and effort now amount to sunk costs.

I witnessed the downside of having invested too much time and effort in a single stock while working at Goldman Sachs. One equity team had a philosophy of focusing on a narrower set of companies and knowing them deeply, including being on a first-name basis with the CEO. Once, during a meeting with the cohead of the investment management division, a member of this team was asked how they defined their job.

The answer they gave was to "be the buy-side axe" on their stocks.[3] When a member of my team was asked the same question, they answered, "Pick stocks that outperform."

An important note about sunk costs is that there can be times when an investment may be partially salvageable, or the least bad alternative is to "finish what you started." As an example, imagine that someone purchased an old house for $200,000, with the plan to spend another $100,000 on remodeling it, for a total investment of $300,000. They expect to be able to sell the refurbished house for $350,000, netting a profit of $50,000. Unfortunately, six months into the effort, they have already blown through the full $100,000 remodeling budget, and there is a collapsing housing market. The revised forecast is $150,000 of total remodeling costs and an ultimate sale price of only $325,000. Let's say that they could cut bait now and sell the unfinished project for $260,000. What is the right decision?

By following economists' advice to focus on "marginal costs," they would be correct to keep going and limit their losses to "only" $25,000.

TABLE 2.1 Sunk costs: When to quit and when to keep going

	Original forecast	Quit	Keep going
Purchase price	$200,000	$200,000	$200,000
Remodeling budget	$100,000	$100,000	$150,000
Full cost	$300,000	$300,000	$350,000
Sale price	$350,000	$260,000	$325,000
Profit/(loss)	**$50,000**	**($40,000)**	**($25,000)**

The CIO of the Value Equity team at Goldman Sachs Asset Management was fond of saying to the investment staff, "Always look forward." It was such a recurring quote that someone eventually had it printed on coffee mugs. The beauty of this phrase is that it leaves unsaid the second half: "Never look backward." It is also incredibly liberating. If you are always looking forward, you let go of any psychological baggage.

Retired Australian golfer Greg Norman, winner of eighty-nine professional tournaments, is nonetheless remembered for the times that he came up short due to excessive nerves or simple bad fortune. In an interview, he described his process for mentally letting go of a bad shot. He said he imagines that he has a toilet and takes all the negative thoughts and emotions, places them in the toilet, then pulls the flush lever. Always look forward.

Another professional athlete, Hall of Fame baseball relief pitcher Trevor Hoffman, once described his process for handling the daily ups and downs of the modern-day closer. After each game, whether he had given up the winning hit or (more often) shut the game down with a strikeout, he would sit alone for a few minutes in the dugout and decompress. If he had performed poorly, he would review his mistakes but then let the bad thoughts and negativity dissipate. If he had performed well, he would enjoy the moment but then talk himself down from his emotional high. When he entered the locker room, the sunk costs and "sunk benefits" were left behind. He might be needed again tomorrow night, so he wanted to have focus and a neutral frame of mind with which to approach the new challenge.

Competitive sports are full of examples of sunk costs and the need to let go of mistakes and misfortune in favor of looking forward to the next play, sequence, or game. The role of professional ice hockey goaltender is perhaps the most intense one in sports. During a hockey game, goalies experience a sustained period of physical, mental, and emotional pressure. While their teammates get regular breaks during line shifts, goalies are on the ice for the full sixty minutes (ignoring occasional tactical decisions to pull the goalie near a game's end). When a goal is scored, the goalie typically gets the lion's share of the blame.

In the immediate aftermath of allowing a goal, goaltenders typically have about one minute before the next face-off. During this time, they need to process any feelings of anger, disappointment, and frustration and reestablish an inner calm and focus. If goalies allow themselves to dwell on the goal or engage in negative self-talk, they risk compounding the problem by being distracted as the puck is dropped and play resumes.

One way in which professional goalies attempt to regain their composure is to use their time off the ice and during practice to prepare themselves for those moments of intensity by developing micromeditation techniques and using mental anchors to reground their minds. For example, former Washington Capitals goalie and Stanley Cup winner Braden Holtby used stoppages during play to focus on a single droplet of condensation on his water bottle.[4] This kept his mind from wandering to the topic of any mistakes that he had made during the last shift.

The methods of avoiding falling victim to sunk-cost fallacy also depend on whether one is acting alone or as part of a group. If acting alone, try the mental techniques used by Norman, Hoffman, and Holtby. In other words, visualize yourself letting go. In a personal journal or diary, write down and acknowledge the mistakes of the past, but then forgive yourself for them.

If acting in concert with others, the group can be effective in helping the individual avoid falling into the sunk-cost fallacy trap. For example, a project that is not going well can be reassigned to someone with a proverbial "fresh set of eyes."

When hedge fund manager Bill Ackman of Pershing Square Capital Management spoke at a Columbia Student Investment Management Association conference several years ago, he described his team's process for developing a new investment idea. He established the working unit as a three-person team in which one individual was the sponsoring analyst, the second was neutral, and the third had the job of undermining the investment case. Ackman expressed concern that an analyst acting alone, who had put six months of effort into developing an idea, would be eager to see it realized. The sunk cost of six months could blind the analyst to the risks involved. Creating a balanced three-person team, with the bear argument assigned to a different individual, dealt with this issue.

SOLUTION SUMMARY

1. **Let it go.** Use the visualization techniques of Norman, Hoffman, and Holtby to let go of past results and focus on the next opportunity.
2. **Always look forward.** Keep the focus on the next opportunity at hand. Consider only the marginal or incremental costs to pursue that opportunity.
3. **Get a fresh perspective.** A project that is not going well can be reassigned, for instance.

Chapter Three

HINDSIGHT BIAS

It is difficult to make predictions, especially about the future.

—Danish proverb, early twentieth century

It is easy to be wise after the event.

—Historical saying, highlighted by Sir Arthur Conan Doyle

AS THE EVENING of November 8, 2016, unfolded, it gradually became apparent that the US presidential race was going to be tighter than most expected. On the day of the election, the *New York Times* election model put Hillary Clinton's chances of victory at 85 percent, and Donald Trump's at 15 percent. The newspaper put Clinton's chance of losing in these terms: "about the same as the probability that an N.F.L. kicker misses a 37-yard field goal."[1] Another way of conceptualizing the odds is that it's just a touch less than the probability of a six coming up on the roll of a die (16.7 percent).

Other predictions put Clinton's chances much higher. The Princeton Election Consortium's statistical Bayesian model, developed by Princeton professor Sam Wang, a neuroscientist and data scientist, put the odds of victory at 99 percent.[2]

The highest published odds for Trump of which I am aware came from Nate Silver's model, whose final estimate on the morning of Election Day gave him a 28.6 percent chance of winning.[3]

I was watching the election coverage on television that night, flipping between news networks. I was also following the live political prediction markets online. Midway through the evening, the betting markets swung strongly in favor of Trump, predicting victory several hours before the networks called the race.

The recriminations and second-guessing of the Clinton campaign's election strategy began late that night and picked up steam the next day. What had gone wrong? The consensus of the experts settled on the observation that the Clinton campaign had neglected the industrial Midwest. In fact, Trump won three states (Michigan, Pennsylvania, and Wisconsin) by less than 1 percent of the vote, which gave him enough Electoral College votes to put him over the top.[4] The criticism was further refined to focus on Clinton's decision not to even make an appearance in the state of Wisconsin, which she lost by less than 23,000 votes.

The observation that Clinton would have won the election if she had won those three states in the Midwest is mathematically true. However, criticizing the campaign's neglect of Wisconsin is a textbook case of hindsight bias.[5]

Hindsight bias occurs when someone believes that the outcome of an event from the past was foreseeable or more predictable than it was at the time. "Hindsight is 20/20" is a phrase that captures the sentiment, as does the retort, "Woulda, coulda, shoulda." It is particularly common in history books, where outcomes are known and the author reasons backward in time to identify important decisions and turning points in battles or wars, for example.

In the case of the 2016 presidential election, a search for newspaper articles written prior to November 8 mentioning the Clinton campaign strategy in Wisconsin turn up no results critical of the Clinton campaign. In fact, the minimal pundit commentary on Wisconsin from before the election consisted of questioning Donald Trump's strategy of campaigning in a state that was such a long shot for him.

The study of hindsight bias can be traced to Baruch Fischhoff.[6] He describes experiments in which subjects were given a description of an unfamiliar historical situation and asked to put probabilities on the likely outcome from four options. Subjects who were told the actual outcome placed a higher probability on that scenario than those who were not informed of the actual outcome. The subjects also underestimated how much the knowledge of the outcome affected their judgment. Fischoff coined the term "creeping determinism" to describe the idea that certain events seem to have been inevitable or preordained if one is aware of the ultimate outcome.

In investment markets, there is a tool that seems to have been custom-designed to encourage hindsight bias: the stock price chart, on which time is plotted on the horizontal axis and price is plotted on the vertical axis. With mathematical precision, every wriggle, zig, and zag in the stock's history is plotted. The chart gives a depiction of the fortune that could have been made. Looking at the price chart of a volatile stock, it is easy to conclude that one would have known exactly when to buy and sell.

Most people, including many professional investors, believe that the goal of investing is to predict the future. When I have appeared on CNBC or Bloomberg Television, I have been asked by the show host a version of, "What will stocks do over the remainder of this year?" I can take a guess at the answer, and in my weaker moments, I may even allow myself to have an opinion. But the truth is that there are too many interacting variables at play in a period of less than one year for anyone to make a reliable prediction.

The unreliability of "expert" forecasts will never stop CNBC anchors or others from asking for one. After all, psychics, crystal ball gazers, tarot card readers, witch doctors, racetrack touts, and those who purport to read animal entrails have been around for a long time. Humans are uncomfortable with uncertainty and have a deep psychological need to know what the future holds. There will always be a market for predictions.

A useful mental model for developing a mindset to evaluate future scenarios is the concept of a multiverse, or multiple universes. Another version of this concept is the "butterfly effect," in which a small change in a dynamic system can produce wildly different outcomes. Maintaining respect for the fragility of the unfolding future can help remind us to be realistic about what was knowable in the past.

A good investment process will document the analyst's opinions, forecasts, and assumptions. Standard fare for written material is an investment thesis; basic numerical information such as price-to-earnings (P/E) ratio, market capitalization, dividend yield, and earnings per share; a company description; and a list of strengths, weaknesses, and risks. Other material will include valuation work culminating in a price target and a model with financial forecasts.

In my experience, most analysts are good at putting things in writing. The problems come when what is written is imprecise and when the material is edited over time, without ever returning to the original documents.

A pet peeve of mine is when a written investment thesis takes the following form: "Company X is a strong company with good products and a capable management team." This statement is likely to be uncontroversial and tells us nothing about why this stock is mispriced or could surprise and produce above-average returns in the future. It will also be very difficult to evaluate whether this thesis will remain valid as the future unfolds. There are no dates or specific metrics to use in an after-the-fact evaluation.

A better investment thesis reads something like this: "Company X is experiencing a temporary downturn in its business that is causing other investors to mistakenly extrapolate. Within two quarters, the company will have launched a new product that will help to increase sales by 15 percent in the next calendar year. In the meantime, management is likely to repurchase at least 10 percent of shares outstanding, which at current valuation levels is accretive to intrinsic value per share." This thesis is specific and has milestones along the way that can be evaluated.

Having a precise, well-written thesis or rationale for owning a stock, along with a valuation model and other written documentation, only has value if one uses it in the future. This is where many professional investors come up short. You must go back and read what you wrote.

One practice that we employed at Eaton Vance was to ask our analysts to update their investment thesis document on an annual basis. Particularly if a stock had been especially strong or weak, it was useful to understand if the thesis had already played out, unraveled, or remained intact. Specifically, I asked our analysts to mark up their original document in red ink, crossing out what was no longer relevant, adding anything new, and indicating what they had gotten wrong or right. They would then present this red-lined document to their colleagues.

This exercise was powerful because it forced the analysts to confront their own words from the time of their original purchase decision. There was nowhere to hide. This was not intended to be a game of "gotcha." In fact, if the analysts wished to make a fresh case for the stock, they were free to do so; they simply were not permitted to allow inertia and "thesis drift" to be the default.

The practice of writing one's decision rationale and then regularly reviewing it as time unfolds is useful for combating hindsight bias. It is difficult to remember the past differently when you are confronted with your own words from the time of the decision. If an alternative perspective was so obvious, why did you not put it in writing at the time?

In addition to reviewing one's investment thesis as time unfolds, using the sell decision as the trigger for a postmortem review can be revealing. I recently joined the Babson College Fund as an executive-in-residence, a role where I mentor and advise undergraduate and postgraduate students in a course in which they manage a portion of the school's endowment. As a component of the investment process, a postmortem write-up is done for each stock as it exits the portfolio. This is true of successes as well as failures. It is important to recognize those situations where the stock went up, but not for the reasons you anticipated.

For stocks that fall 20 percent or more, but where the students wish to continue to hold or add to the position, it must be "re-underwritten." Importantly, this task must be performed by a different student from the one who originally presented it. This simple zero-based review has the effect of simultaneously combating the first three biases that we have discussed (endowment effect, sunk-cost fallacy, and hindsight bias).

SOLUTION SUMMARY

1. **Write it down.** Put your forecasts and assumptions in writing. Regularly review what you have written and acknowledge when you are adjusting your assumptions. Do not overwrite the old work; retain the prior forecast and write a separate, new one to update it.
2. **Don't believe your lyin' eyes.** Be wary of overusing stock price charts and any other visual illustrations of the past. Their precision can give a false sense of what was knowable or preordained.
3. **Conduct a postmortem.** Review past forecasts (which of course were made in writing). Acknowledge what you got right and what you got wrong. Be sure to debrief on successes as well as failures. Focus on what was knowable at the time, not in hindsight.

Chapter Four

OUTCOME BIAS

To go wrong in one's own way is better than to go right in someone else's.

—Fyodor Dostoevsky, *Crime and Punishment*

Worldly wisdom teaches that it is better for reputation to fail conventionally than to succeed unconventionally.

—John Maynard Keynes, British economist

OUTCOME BIAS occurs when we judge the quality of a decision with knowledge of the outcome rather than considering what was known at the time that the decision was made.[1] I had the opportunity to witness outcome bias up close in the National Football League (NFL) in the late 1990s.

On the afternoon of September 17, 1995, my favorite team, the San Diego Chargers, were on the road against the Philadelphia Eagles. They fell behind 14–0 before scoring a touchdown to make it 14–6 pending the extra point, which the Chargers made. The Chargers went on to win the game, but something about that extra-point decision nagged at me for the rest of the day.

Since the Chargers had trailed by two touchdowns, they needed two seven-point touchdowns to tie and eventually send the game to overtime, assuming that all other scoring was equal between the two teams. What if the Chargers had attempted a two-point conversion instead? Obviously, a successful two-point conversion followed by a second touchdown with a one-point conversion would give them the win. Less obviously, a missed two-point conversion would not automatically give them a loss. This is because a failed conversion could be followed by a second attempt at a two-point conversion after the next touchdown, which, if successful, would have the effect of salvaging the overtime scenario. Only the case of consecutive two-point conversion misses would leave them worse off than the conventional approach of attempting a kick.

Many of the insights from sports analytics take the form of failure being less bad than assumed. For example, a team that fails in its attempt on fourth-and-goal from the opponent's one-yard line is awarded the consolation prize of pinning the other team's offense against its own end zone. Possessing the ball inside your own ten-yard line is worth negative expected points.[2]

Three years after the Chargers game that had piqued my interest, I undertook a deep level of research on the two-point conversion topic. I learned that several NFL coaches relied on a conversion chart that had been drawn up by Dick Vermeil when he was coaching at the University of California, Los Angeles (UCLA) in the early 1970s. I obtained a copy of the chart and identified several errors in it, including the "down eight points after scoring" scenario.

I set about building an updated, accurate conversion decision chart for use in the NFL. In the four seasons since the two-point option was introduced, it had succeeded 44.5 percent of the time, while one-point attempts had a success rate of 95.5 percent.

The Product Rule of Probability states that the probability of a series of independent events is the product of all the individual event probabilities. In other words, multiply the odds together to get the overall odds. For example, when flipping coins, the odds of getting heads three times in a row is one-in-eight, calculated as follows: 50% x 50% x 50% = 12.5% (1/8).

Using this concept for the NFL conversion probabilities produced the calculations that are shown in figures 4.1 and 4.2. Figure 4.1 shows the calculations for the conventional approach of attempting an extra-point kick. Figure 4.2 shows the "enlightened" approach of going for two points.[3]

In other words, the unconventional, enlightened strategy of going for two points actually improved the team's chances of victory from 46.6 percent to 55.8 percent—a significant margin.

Prior to the 1998 NFL season, I decided to mail a letter advocating a quantitative approach to in-game decisions to every team owner in the NFL. Over the next two weeks, I received six reply letters. Four of them were various forms of polite rejection. Two other letters, one from Lamar Hunt, owner of the Kansas City Chiefs, the other from Bud Adams, owner of the Tennessee Oilers (later renamed the Titans), expressed nibbles of interest.

Phone calls to the Tennessee Oilers' headquarters led to a meeting with general manager (GM) Floyd Reese in Nashville. In addition to the conversion chart, I was prepared to discuss other areas of analytical opportunity, including fourth-down decisions, clock and time-out management, end-game theory, and other outside-the-box ideas.[4]

Bill James had helped develop the study of baseball analytics, culminating in the coining of the term "sabermetrics" in 1980. As far as I knew at the time of my meeting in November 1998,

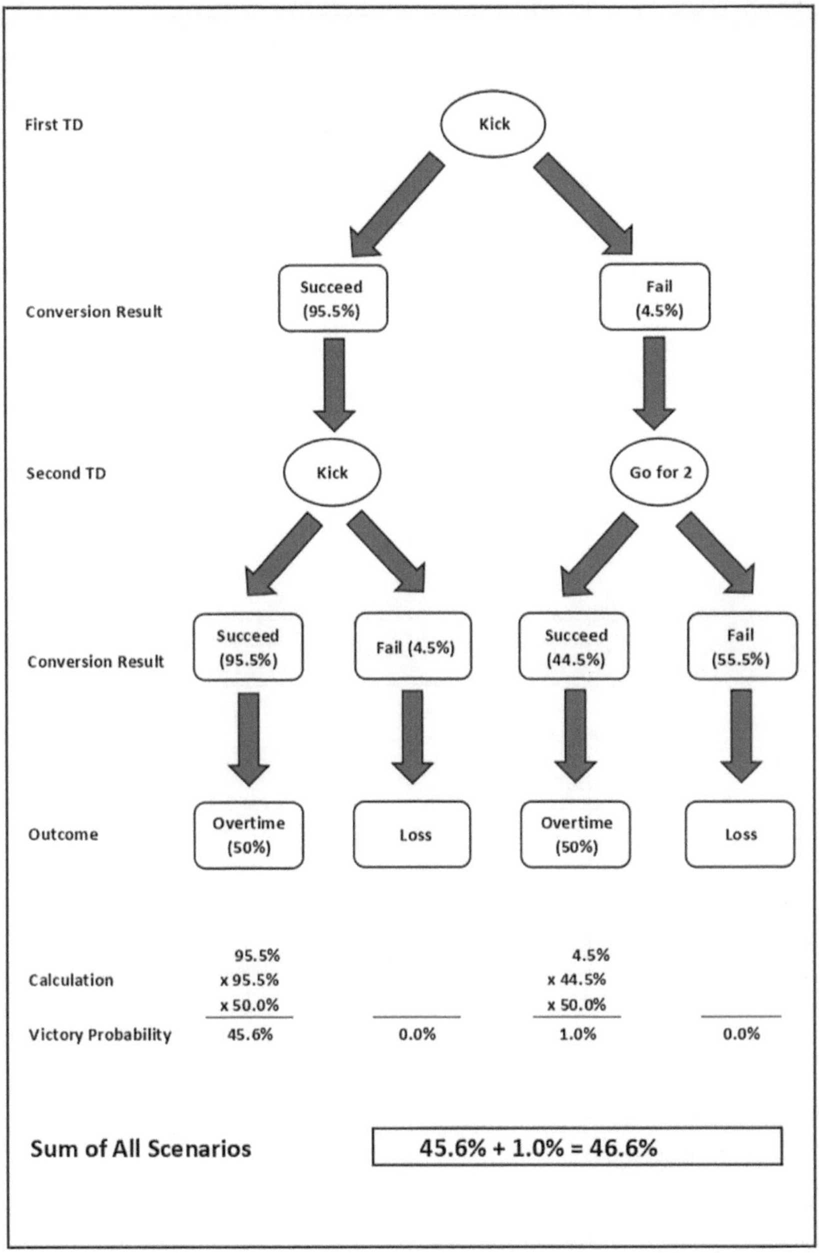

FIGURE 4.1 Conversion decision after scoring a touchdown (TD) to go down 8 points: conventional approach (Kick).

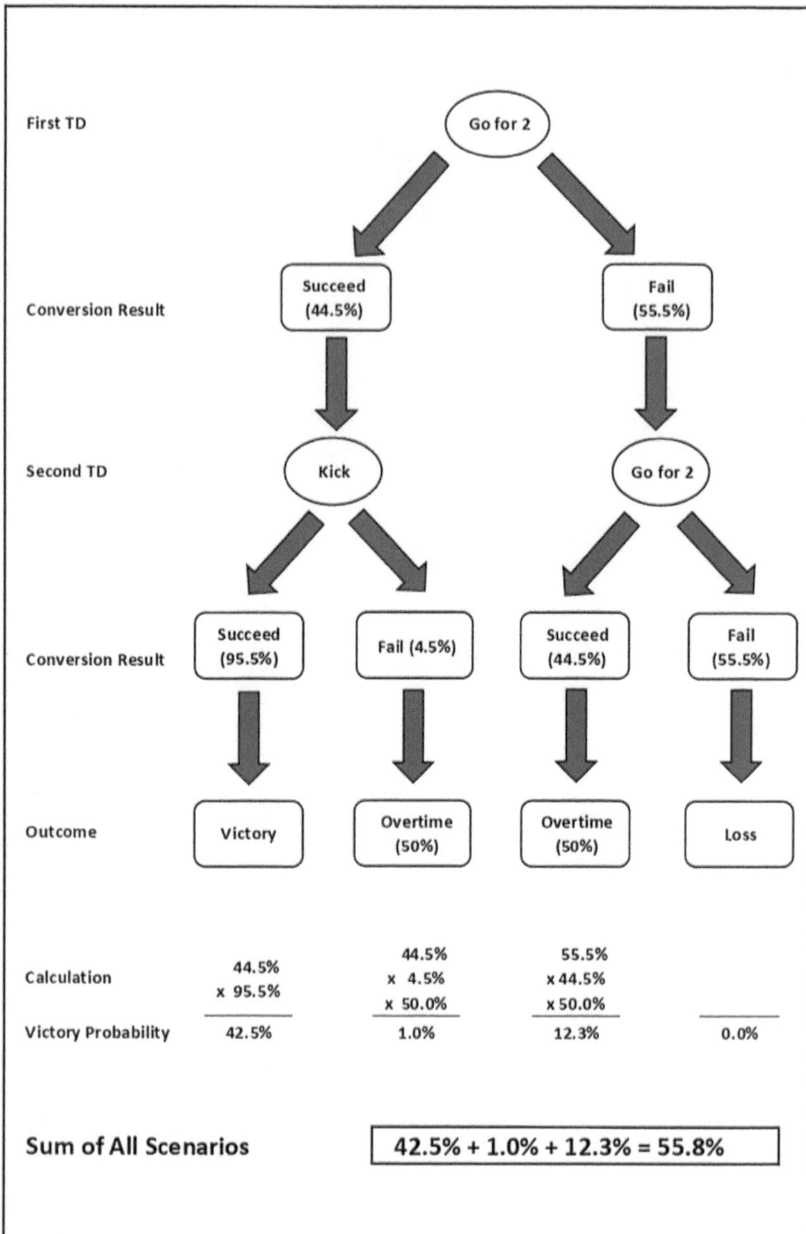

FIGURE 4.2 Conversion decision after scoring a TD to go down 8 points: enlightened approach (Go for 2).

no similar depth of sports analytics had been done for football, and yet here I was, pitching an NFL GM on how to make better decisions during a game, using math!

On the day of our meeting, the vibe in the office was upbeat; after starting the season 1–3, the team had turned things around and were sitting on a winning record (5–4) for the first time that year, after a road win against Tampa Bay two days prior.

The GM and I spoke at a high level about the importance of having a forward-thinking, unconventional mindset. "I can remember when coaches thought it would make players tougher to deny them water during practice," he said.

We spoke for nearly three hours. Toward the end of our conversation, we had moved beyond the question of the value of what I was proposing to the topic of protecting the intellectual property that it represented.

"Eddie, you have to understand how tight-knit the world of football is," the GM shared. If I were to hire you or buy your conversion chart, here is what would happen. We give the chart to [the head coach] Jeff Fisher. He hands it to an assistant coach. That assistant coach faxes it to his brother-in-law, who coaches in the college game. By week eight, every team in the NFL would have your chart."

We followed up with a lengthy phone call three weeks later, but I could not close the deal. Unfortunately, numerous calls to Lamar Hunt's office did not yield a meeting with the Chiefs.

Many years later, in March 2020, at the MIT Sloan Sports Analytics Conference, I sat in the audience as Bill James, the legend himself, was interviewed. He said that simply having a good idea or insight is not enough. In his experience, it takes the established order about ten years to embrace a new concept. Even that may be too optimistic. It has now been more than a quarter century since I shared my insights with the Tennessee Oilers; the logic of the down-eight-points decision is now universally accepted within the sports analytics community. Nonetheless, many NFL coaches still opt for the flawed, conventional approach when down by eight points.

Conventional decision making in the NFL is reinforced by second-guessing, a form of outcome bias. After a narrow loss, coaches are immediately subjected to a mandatory press conference with reporters who want to know what went wrong. Over the ensuing days, local radio, podcasts, newspapers, and social media mercilessly judge every decision with the benefit of knowing its outcome. This is not a backdrop that encourages coaches to think independently.

A good example of second-guessing followed the NFL Divisional playoff game between the Tampa Bay Buccaneers and the Detroit Lions on January 21, 2024. In the fourth quarter, Tampa Bay was down fourteen points and scored a touchdown to put themselves down eight, the same situation that I had evaluated twenty-five years earlier. Head coach Todd Bowles elected to go for a two-point conversion, which the television announcers noted was correct according to the analytics, but the conversion attempt failed. The next day on ESPN's *Pardon the Interruption*, cohost Michael Wilbon went on a rant:

> The two-point conversion attempt that left them eight down, don't start me with the two-point conversion. The analytics say go for it. Do the analytics say go for it no matter

> who's going for it? So, if you and I were on the field, the analytics say go for it? It's the stupidest, laziest, lamest thing I've ever heard for reasoning in competition. And I hate when announcers buy it without questioning it.[5]

It is true that the analytics calculations typically use leaguewide averages to develop a baseline from a larger sample size. It is also true that if the Buccaneers' two-point chances had been sufficiently low, then a one-point conversion would have been the right decision. However, to move off the general recommendation of a two-point conversion, the Bucs' offensive personnel would have needed a two-point conversion success rate below 35 percent (compared to the leaguewide average success rate of 55 percent for the 2023 season).

It is not surprising, then, that the best-known cliché to describe outcome bias comes from the game of football. "Monday morning quarterbacks" are know-it-alls who have all the answers . . . after the fact.

I believe that the solution for NFL teams is for the owner to take responsibility and be willing to shoulder the blame. He or she should hire a head coach who understands the importance of quantitative analytics and has the backbone to execute unconventional strategies and decisions. Incentives to take the unconventional approach should be built into the coach's contract. Upon hiring this enlightened individual, the owner should hold a press conference and give a version of the following speech:

> This team aspires to be the most forward-thinking in the league in its use of analytics. Our new head coach believes

in this strategy, and I will be holding him accountable for it. The effect of this approach is that we will be doing unconventional things throughout the season that may look very odd without context. These will include personnel decisions, travel plans, in-game strategy, draft-day trades, etc. These decisions, though well considered, will not work out in certain instances. In the long run, I expect them to help us become a championship organization. The job security of our new head coach will be unaffected by the short-term result of any unconventional, but sound decision. All criticism should be directed at me.

Postscript: On January 30, 2000, just over fourteen months after my meeting in Nashville, the newly renamed Tennessee Titans made it to Super Bowl XXXIV, where they lost to the St. Louis Rams by a score of 23–16. The game famously came down to the final play, in which Titans wide receiver Kevin Dyson was tackled by Rams linebacker Mike Jones one yard short of the goal line as time expired. The Titans had burned a time-out to avoid a five-yard delay-of-game penalty late in the third quarter, which would prove to be immeasurably costly. In my less humble moments, I allow myself to imagine an alternative universe in which I implemented an improved clock management system for the team that properly valued—and preserved—that time-out, leading to a Super Bowl victory for the Tennessee Titans.

Beyond the world of sports, I like to illustrate outcome bias by asking this absurd question: "Suppose that someone puts a blindfold on and slowly walks across a busy highway with fast-moving cars. Assuming that this person makes it to the other side unharmed, was that a good decision?" The evaluation of a decision must be made independent of the result. However, as humans, we are not wired to do this.

With outcome bias, the individual judges the quality of a decision by factoring in the knowledge of how the decision turned out. It is possible that the decision was perfectly sound, given the information that the decision-maker had at the time, but unforeseen events or simple dumb luck produced a poor outcome.[6] Likewise, a poor decision may be glossed over if the outcome turns out all right. Figure 4.3 suggests the correct conclusion to draw from different process-versus-outcome combinations.

FIGURE 4.3 Judging decision quality.

Source: This two-by-two decision-quality matrix is a modified version of a concept developed by J. Edward Russo and Paul J. H. Schoemaker and later popularized by Annie Duke.

To identify and research outcome bias, researchers conducted five experiments in which they presented hypothetical scenarios with varied outcomes to their subjects.[7] The scenarios involved decisions regarding different, risky medical decisions and variations of modest-sized monetary gambles. Different subjects were given the same front-end information and probability of success, but some subjects were told that the decision succeeded, while others were told that it failed. Those who were told that the decision failed judged the quality of the decision to be worse than those who were told that it succeeded.

Outcome bias can occur due to ignoring mean reversion. Reversion to the mean is a concept from statistics that acknowledges that over a small number of trials, outlier events can occur, such as flipping a coin and having it come up heads several times in a row. However, over many trials, the results will approach (regress toward) a mean or average. The mark of a good predictive model is that it will test well out of sample. In other words, the model is not relying on the outcomes from the data set that was used for its construction.

In addition to sports, outcome bias is prevalent in investment markets and many other facets of life. With the benefit of the outcome in hand, it is easy to cast blame, particularly when the conventional decision would have yielded a better result in a particular circumstance.

Investment consultants, oversight boards, due diligence analysts, and others who are charged with evaluating the skill of portfolio managers should recognize the shortcomings of overemphasizing the outcome. The temptation to study a short-term performance track record is high, but the best approach is likely one that blends a subjective assessment with the hard numbers, which likely contain much noise.

At a debate with Warren Buffett in 1984, Michael Jensen, an academic who believed in the efficient market hypothesis (EMH), described the metaphor of a nationwide contest of people calling heads or tails for a series of coin flips. Inevitably, he argued, some small number of people would get twenty calls in a row correct. But that could all be explained by chance.[8]

Buffett, an opponent of the EMH, took Jensen's metaphor and modified it. Buffett countered that chance would be an unlikely explanation if all the correct coin-flip callers came from the same small town. In the case of beating the stock market, this would be the intellectual village of "Graham and Doddsville."[9] Benjamin Graham and David Dodd taught at Columbia University and wrote *Security Analysis*, the seminal text on value investing. In other words, the outsized success of the concepts from value investing applied across markets, asset classes, and individual securities had borne fruit that could not be explained by chance.

Outcome bias can lead to unfair outcomes. For example, malpractice lawsuits may be brought against doctors who make decisions that are perfectly sound, given the information that they have at their disposal, but where the outcome happens to turn out badly. Coaches and managers of professional sports teams may lose their jobs after a poor run of performance that is due to a short-term statistical anomaly resulting from events outside their control. Mean reversion will tend to make the firing decision look wise as the team inevitably bounces back from a period of temporary underperformance.

Skillful gamblers understand the concept of differentiating between a good/bad decision and a good/bad outcome. For example, in a Texas hold 'em poker game, suppose that a player faces the decision to call or fold before the final "river" card is dealt. There is $50 in the pot, and the player must call a $10 bet to stay in the hand. The "pot odds" are said to be 5-to-1 ($50 potential win for a $10 bet). There are four upturned cards on the table ("the board") and two known cards in the player's own hand. That leaves forty-six unseen cards from the fifty-two-card deck. Suppose that the player is hoping to hit an inside straight; there are four cards left that would give a wining hand. The odds of winning are 42-to-4 (i.e., 10.5-to-1), and yet the pot odds are only 5-to-1. The correct move is to fold.[10] If the player calls, that is a bad decision even if one of those four winning cards is ultimately turned over on the table.

My teenage son recently discovered Texas hold 'em and plays in a regular, low-stakes game with his friends. He told me that when they make a tough fold, several of his friends will ask the dealer to deal out the remaining cards to see "what would have happened" had they remained in the pot.[11] They either take solace in their decision or berate themselves, depending on the outcome. I think that this is a poor practice because it reinforces outcome bias.

In *The Theory of Poker*, author David Sklansky uses the term "getting the best of it" to describe the concept of making a decision that is optimal in the long run or, alternatively, having an opponent make a poor long-run decision, regardless of how it turns out in the current instance. Here, "long-run" refers not to a long period of time but the idea of how the scenario would turn out on average if simulated many times.

The purchase of insurance is another area where outcome bias is prevalent. People will complain that they have wasted money for many years paying premiums to insurance companies despite never having a claim. The soundness of the decision to purchase insurance should be judged at the time that the policy is taken out, weighing the cost versus the likelihood and size of a potential future claim, not after the results are in and the risk fails to materialize.

SOLUTION SUMMARY

1. **Test out of sample.** When evaluating a data set in search of cause-and-effect relationships, avoid being tricked by spurious correlations that lead to faulty conclusions influenced by outcome bias.
2. **Reward the process.** Leaders should evaluate and reward good processes rather than good outcomes, particularly when there is a heavy component of luck versus skill.
3. **Get the best of it.** When evaluating the quality of a decision, study whether the decision maker got the best of it. Was the decision optimal if the scenario were simulated 1,000 times?

Chapter Five

SURVIVORSHIP BIAS

The future is unwritten.
—Joe Strummer, lead vocalist of the Clash

History will be kind to me, for I intend to write it.
—Winston Churchill, UK prime minister (1940–1945 and 1951–1955)

ON FEBRUARY 15, 1983, PBS aired "The Miracle of Life," an episode of *Nova*, a show that explores scientific discoveries. It was the most-watched *Nova* documentary ever made, came to be used in school classrooms for sex education, and had an influence on how a generation of people understood human reproduction. The documentary depicts the fertilization process in detail, and one is left with the impression that the sperm's journey to the egg is a perilous one. Of the 250 million sperm that make the trip, only one can be the successful survivor.

Each of us is unique, and our individual existence is a story of long odds. For those who do not subscribe to theories of fate or destiny, things could easily have turned out very differently. Whether it's our own existence or something more mundane, when looking at the past, it is natural to reason backward from the end point. When we do this, we risk concluding that outcomes were inevitable, or missing possibilities that were present but did not come to fruition.

During World War II, Abraham Wald worked in support of the war effort on behalf of the Statistical Research Group at Columbia University. His group studied planes returning from bombing campaigns. They evaluated the location of the aircrafts' bullet holes to determine where to place protective armor. Figure 5.1 illustrates a hypothetical returning aircraft with bullet holes in various locations. Wald's counterintuitive contribution was to point out that armor ought to be placed on the engines, which showed little damage to the aircraft that they studied, but where the planes that had not returned had

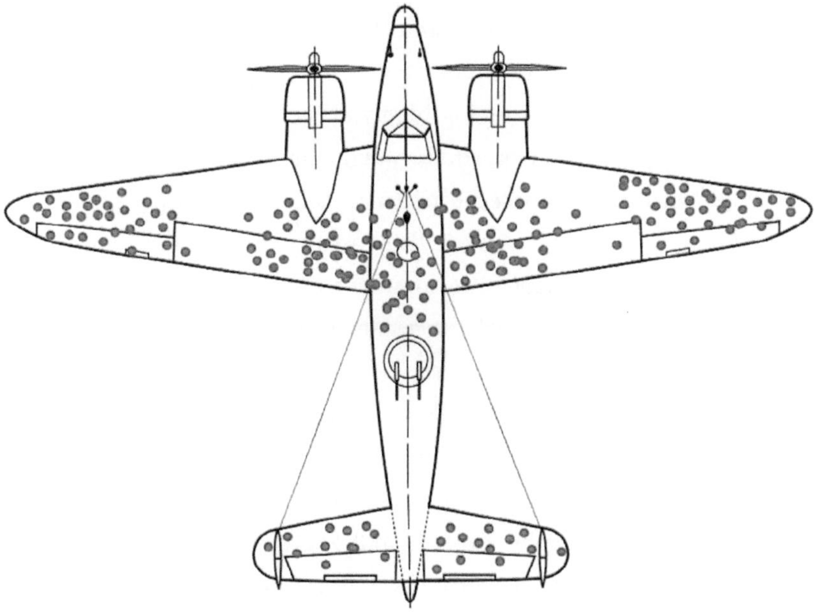

FIGURE 5.1 A surviving plane riddled with bullets.

Source: Martin Grandjean and McGeddon, *Survivorship-bias.svg*, Wikimedia Commons, 2021, licensed under CC BY-SA 4.0, https://commons.wikimedia.org/wiki/File:Survivorship-bias.svg

likely been hit. In other words, he recognized that the aircraft that they were studying (i.e., planes that had survived) were not the full data set.[1]

Survivorship bias is rampant in professional investing circles. Over time, underperforming funds are closed or merged. Portfolio managers and investment analysts who have a tough run lose their jobs. The survivors look good because the laggards have been eliminated from the averages.[2]

A cynic once suggested to me that the easiest path to success for a new asset management firm would be to do the following. First, launch ten new funds with seed capital to start the clock on performance track records. Make sure that each of the funds is different from the others and that the tracking error versus the relevant benchmark index for each is very high.[3] This can be accomplished by running highly concentrated portfolios or by having significant portfolio weight invested in nonbenchmark securities. In baseball parlance, this startup firm should "swing for the fences." Wait three years, which is the typical minimum performance measurement period that prospective clients require. Inevitably, the results of these ten funds will be all over the place, but there should be at least one or two that have performed phenomenally well over the period. Next, close all the funds with poor or mediocre performance. Take the one or two funds that have strong track records and market the heck out of them, raising hundreds of millions (or billions) of dollars on which to charge a management fee. Once the money has been raised, neutralize the portfolio by diversifying and reducing tracking error to get much closer to the benchmark to minimize the possibility of a poor performance period in the future, which would lead to the client assets leaving the fund. Sit back and collect fees into perpetuity.

Obviously, the preceding business plan is unethical. If it were done to the extent described, it would easily be spotted by a consultant or other sophisticated observer. However, it illustrates the pernicious effect of survivorship bias. People tend to ignore what cannot be seen, and if the loser funds have been closed, they will go unnoticed by most people.

It is a well-understood concept in finance that risk and return should go together. If markets are efficient, investors demand a higher expected return as compensation for taking on higher levels of risk. For those who believe in the efficient market hypothesis (EMH), it is easy to erroneously extrapolate this concept into the faulty belief that one can always hit the investment return target by simply taking on more risk. For those of us who are skeptical of market efficiency, our search is for investments that produces high returns with low levels of risk. Unfortunately, the opposite type of investment also exists. During speculative bubbles such as Japan in 1989, internet stocks in 2000, and housing or bank stocks in 2008, an investment at the peak represented both high risk and low reward.

The annual compound return on US stocks since 1900 has been just below 10 percent.[4] Financial advisors and investment committees will often use an expected return estimate for US stocks that is anchored to that 10 percent historical figure. For example, the average assumed rate of return on assets for state pension plans was recently 6.87 percent.[5] Since these plans have a mixture of assets (e.g., public equities, fixed income, and real estate) with the typical yield on fixed income below 7 percent, the arithmetic implies an expectation of high single digits, approaching 10 percent, for stocks.

By using a historical data set that goes back more than 120 years, it would be easy to be comforted by the idea that the sample size is sufficiently large and long term. However, one problem with assuming a 10 percent forward-looking return for US stocks is that it does not take account of the conditions that were in place to produce the historical results.

If we imagine climbing into a time machine and going back to the year 1900, we can attempt to step into the shoes of someone alive at that time, contemplating an investment in US stocks. At that time, the United Kingdom had the largest share (24.2 percent) of the global stock market. The United States was a little over half of that level, at 14.4 percent, with Germany close behind, at 12.6 percent.[6] An investor, particularly one based outside the United States, could have very easily decided to invest in the German stock market rather than the US one. In doing so, that investor would have exposed themself to being wiped out when the German market was closed at the onset of World War I, followed by a period of hyperinflation that made the German mark worthless in the 1920s.

In fact, the United States has been the second-best-performing stock market in the world since 1900, trailing only Australia.[7] It might be possible to convince oneself that, standing there in 1900, it would have been easy to see that the United States would come out ahead and a country that was a little more than 120 years old at the time was destined to produce a nice, round 10 percent annual return for its stock market over the ensuing

120 years. But those 1900-era investors would likely have sought regional diversification away from the United States if they had been told to expect that it would be involved in two world wars and two global pandemics, as well as periods of high inflation and economic boom and bust.

History could have taken other paths. In the one that it did take, the investor in German stocks lost everything and the investor in US stocks did very well. The performance of the S&P 500 is flattered by survivorship bias, and people tend to ignore the performance of the German stock market in the early 1900s when discussing the likely return from global equities.

Survivorship bias can be found wherever there is a success story. People understandably want to know what led to success, so they typically start by identifying the winner or best in class in a particular endeavor and then study the history that led to that success. A mountain climber made it to the summit of Everest . . . what was her training regimen? A National Basketball Association (NBA) player wins the Most Valuable Player (MVP) award . . . how many hours of practice did he have in his youth, and what type of coaching did he receive? A technology start-up company made it big . . . how did it do it?

In each of these cases, we are reasoning backward, starting with a data set that includes only the survivors or winners. At first blush, this may seem reasonable; why study the losers? But the reason to study the losers or nonsurvivors is that they may have used the same methods as the survivors, in which case the diagnosis would be incomplete or inaccurate.

SOLUTION SUMMARY

1. **Reason forward, not backward.** Start your analysis at the beginning of the race, not with the winner who happened to cross the finish line first.
2. **Identify the full universe.** When studying a sample, ensure that it is not one that has survived or cleared some prior hurdle or filter.
3. **Study the losers.** Evaluate whether those who failed in an endeavor employed some of the same practices as those who succeeded.

Chapter Six

THE FRAMING EFFECT

Cinema is a matter of what's in the frame and what's out.
—Martin Scorsese, film director

He who frames the question wins the debate.
—Randall Terry, political activist

YOUR FRIEND Tom enjoys betting on sports. He has been the commissioner of a fantasy football league for two decades, occasionally winning the league and its $500 first place prize himself. He studies the National Football League (NFL) draft each year and has strong opinions about which general managers (GMs) are making mistakes, particularly the one for his favorite team. He seems to know all the players, including which rookies are likely to perform well. During the season, he tracks the injury news carefully. Despite all this knowledge and effort, he loses money each season when he bets on NFL games.

This year, he has decided to invest in a paid professional "pick" service. His feed on X serves up regular offers from handicappers with seemingly impressive records. He shows you a few and asks you which one you think he should select:

- "9 of last 11 picks have been winners!"
- "80 percent hit rate on Best Bets this season!"
- "8 for 9 this year on Monday Night Football!"

Hopefully, your advice is some form of "Save your money." Even if these result statements have been verified, there remain several reasons to be skeptical. First, the sample size of each is too small to prove skill. It would require hundreds of picks to determine if skill was a factor. Second, survivorship bias is at work. There are likely other touts who have had a poor run recently, but they aren't mentioning their records. Third, there is cherry picking—why are we talking about only the last eleven picks, "best bets," and Monday Night Football? What about all the other recommendations?

Tom is the victim of clever framing by touts looking to sell him picks. If they were any good, they would bet themselves or partner with a professional bettor with a large bankroll.

The way in which a concept is framed can have a big impact on the way that it is perceived. In fact, the same data presented in two different ways can yield opposite conclusions or decisions.

Amos Tversky and Daniel Kahneman, who had identified the bias of loss aversion in *Prospect Theory*, expanded on the concept in 1981 in a follow-up article in *Science* magazine.[1] They demonstrated that an identical set of facts presented as either a potential loss or potential gain yielded different decisions from their subjects.

Their experiment, titled "The Asia Disease Problem," set up the following premise:

Imagine that the U.S. is preparing for the outbreak of an unusual Asian disease, which is expected to kill 600 people. Two alternative programs to combat the disease have been proposed. Assume that the exact scientific estimate of the consequences of the programs are as follows:

The subjects were divided into two groups. The first group was asked to choose between Programs A and B:

- **Program A**: If Program A is adopted, 200 people will be saved.
- **Program B**: If Program B is adopted, there is a 1/3 probability that 600 people will be saved and a 2/3 probability that no people will be saved.

The second group was asked to choose between Programs C and D:

- **Program C**: If Program C is adopted, 400 people will die.
- **Program D**: If Program D is adopted, there is a 1/3 probability that nobody will die and a 2/3 probability that 600 people will die.

Although Programs A and C are mathematically identical, choice A was selected by 72 percent of participants in group 1, but choice C was picked by just 22 percent of participants in group 2. Likewise, B and D are mathematically the same, but B was selected by only 28 percent of the group, whereas D was picked by 78 percent.

The conclusion that the researchers drew is that people are more willing to take on risk to avoid a loss than to achieve a gain, and when things are framed in terms of loss avoidance, the option has more appeal.

Other researchers have shown that medical decisions can differ depending on the presentation format.[2]

It is not difficult to see how the framing effect applies in an investment setting. For example, an investor focused on avoiding losses will be willing to take more risk than one focused on seeking gains. This effect also reinforces other biases, such as the endowment effect and sunk-cost fallacy.

As a buy-side investor in the asset management industry, I found myself often having investment ideas pitched to me. This pitch could come from a sell-side brokerage analyst or strategist who was pitching a stock or idea in hopes of receiving trading commissions or other forms of payment for research services. Or it could come from a corporate executive who was selling stock in an initial public offering, raising funds in a secondary offering, or simply trying to maintain a high valuation for their outstanding shares. Whether it was a sell-side broker or member of a corporate management team, there was often a pitch deck with compelling visuals.

Investors love to look at charts. This could be the chart of a particular stock's historical price. It may be a graph showing the relationship between two economic variables. When the chart had been put together by a brokerage analyst or a company's investor relations team, I would take it upon myself to look for any spin or tricks they were playing with the data. What time series was chosen? If they were showing me a time period that was odd, such as 6.25 years, why did they select that date range? Was there an event or rationale to explain the start date, or was that simply the date that framed the information in the best possible light? Was the axis of the graph distorted in some way? Sometimes one or both axes would not start at zero, which distorts the image. What were the dimensions of the chart itself? A chart stretched wide across the page or screen suggests a very different conclusion from the same one using square dimensions.

The two bar charts in figures 6.1 and 6.2 show customer satisfaction scores for the year 2025 from the American Customer Satisfaction Index (ACSI) survey of quick service restaurants (QSRs). The data in both charts is mathematically accurate, but the charts are framed to tell two different stories. In the first chart, a subset of the QSR category is used. Also, the vertical axis plots scores from 69 to 79. This has the effect of making

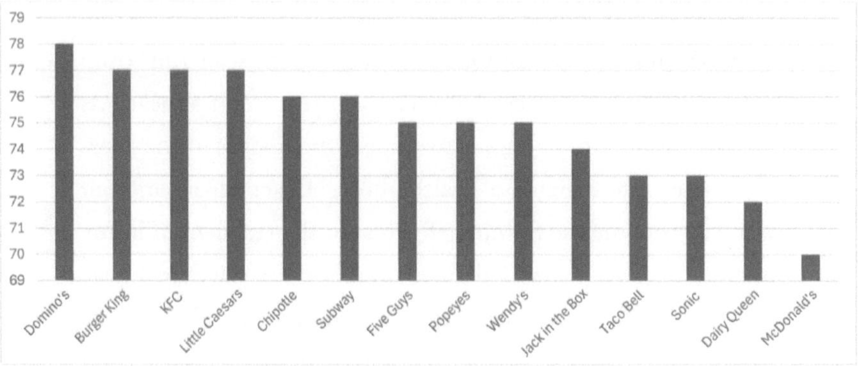

FIGURE 6.1 Customer satisfaction at quick-service restaurants.
Source: American Customer Satisfaction Index (ACSI, 2025).

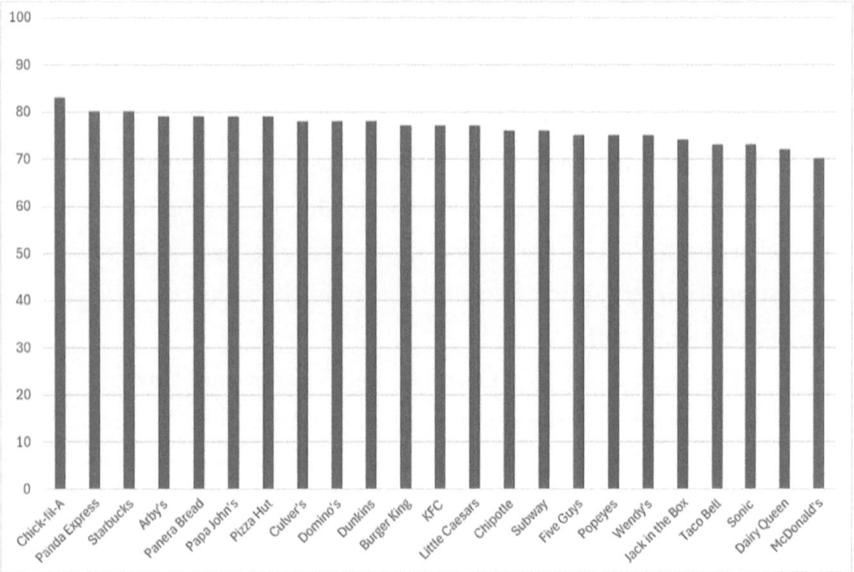

FIGURE 6.2 Customer satisfaction at quick-service restaurants.
Source: American Customer Satisfaction Index (ACSI, 2025).

Domino's Pizza appear to be the top restaurant. In the second chart, the full universe of QSRs is used and the scale runs from 0 to 100. The differences between each restaurant appear less extreme, and Domino's finds itself near the middle of the pack.

Besides internalizing a healthy dose of skepticism, another way to overcome the framing effect is for the recipient of information to insist on a well-defined template. For example, I have seen independent trustees of mutual fund boards, who provide fiduciary oversight on behalf of fund shareholders, insist that materials from portfolio managers include a cover sheet with pertinent information of the trustees' choosing. This checklist of information would be very specifically defined. For example, the performance had to be shown for a predetermined period as of a predetermined date. This took away the option for the presenter to cherry-pick the data that looked the best.

Framing is a tool that a counterparty, marketer, or salesperson can use to encourage you to make a transaction, but investors may also mislead themselves by how they choose to frame things. Investing is complex. There is an enormous amount of information available for every public company. In addition, the generally accepted accounting principles (GAAP) can be overly detailed or misleading. So it is understandable that investors want to simplify things for themselves. It is important, however, that in this winnowing, simplification process, truth and insight are not lost.

Valuation ratios are one way in which simplification can lead one astray. For example, a popular metric is enterprise value/earnings before interest, taxes, depreciation, and amortization (EV/EBITDA), which is the market value of the entire capital structure of the enterprise, including equity, debt, convertibles, preferred stock less any excess cash divided by earnings before interest, tax, depreciation, and amortization expenses. Certain investors will even use the denominator, EBITDA, as shorthand for cash flow. However, EBITDA does not give warranted credit to companies with structurally lower tax rates, and adding back depreciation without subtracting a charge for maintenance capital expenditures gives a false impression of sustainable cash flow levels.

In 2007, about a year before the global financial crisis fully unfolded, I attended a group investor meeting with the management of the real estate company Prologis. Prologis was an industrial real estate investment trust (REIT) that owned warehouses and distribution centers benefiting from global trade. Much of the conversation centered around its expansion plans in China. Prologis was a darling of Wall Street; it was viewed as a high-quality growth company. I had a different opinion; I did not fully trust the management team and found the financial statements to be indecipherable. They had numerous joint ventures (JVs) that were heavily leveraged and kept debt off the reported balance sheet. At one point in the group conversation, one of the hedge fund analysts asked the management team why they weren't buying back stock. The answer was, "We don't want to push our leverage levels too much further." The analyst gasped and responded, "But you are so underleveraged." Several of the other analysts around the table nodded and looked confused by management's answer. These investors measured indebtedness using debt/EV. There were two problems with framing things this way: It ignored the debt embedded in the JVs, and it used the company's elevated share price (market cap is a component of EV) in the denominator. This was a light bulb moment for me, as I had previously been concerned that I was being too cynical about how I was perceiving the company and its financial health. Over the next eighteen months, the stock price collapsed by 80 percent.

I have also seen professional investors fail to think through how revenues and expenses are related. A company announces a 5 percent reduction in staff, and the eager analyst plugs the cost savings into the earnings model without stopping to think whether any of the firm's revenues were supported (even indirectly) by the employees who will be leaving.

Another form of revenue growth versus expense mismatch is in capital expenditures. I have reviewed many earnings and cash flow models that show an improved top line with no corresponding rise in capital spending or depreciation expenses. This is fantastic if it is true, but count me as a skeptic that a mature company can alter its capital efficiency overnight. If we break down revenues into price multiplied by units, then revenues can rise from a change in either of those two variables. If units go up, surely there will eventually be a need for new workers and equipment to support growth. If price goes up, then so-called operating leverage is more believable, but assumptions of pricing power should be met with skepticism. Will customers look for a substitute? Will competitors at lower price points take market share?

I often hear investors, particularly when they are in a marketing mood, talk about the huge cash pile that investors are holding. This argument is typically framed like this: "With $7 trillion of cash sitting on the sidelines, any improvement in investor confidence will lead to a flood of money into stocks and bonds, pushing up prices." This type of framing conjures up images of a large river flowing downstream until it pours over a cliff edge, violently plunging hundreds of feet like Victoria Falls.

Before we fully embrace this mental frame, let's "work through the T accounts," as our accounting friends might say. If a particular individual investor takes $1,000 in cash and uses it to buy a stock, what happens to that cash? Well, there is another investor who sells and receives the cash, so the market's overall cash level is unchanged. What if the investor puts the money into a mutual fund? The T-account analysis tells us that the fund manager will spend that cash on a stock and the same result will occur. What if a brand-new company is formed, which raises cash from investors for operating purposes? First, that cash will initially go into the new company's bank account and as it spends the money on wages, material, and equipment, those recipients will put the cash into their own bank accounts, maintaining the economy's overall cash level. Second, the company represents new supply to the investment markets, so it negates the "flows will drive asset prices" argument. Bottom line, in the United States, the government authorities (the Federal Reserve and US Department of the Treasury) determine how much cash to put into the economy, and that balance will not change based on how market participants pass it around among themselves.[3]

Clichés and heuristics are a form of framing. These are all over the place on Wall Street, and it is easy to adopt them as a shorthand way of describing a situation. Here are just a few that immediately come to mind:

- Don't catch a falling knife.
- The stock market rides the escalator up but takes the elevator down.
- The setup looks good.
- Another "beat and raise" quarter.
- Headline risk.
- Buy low, sell high.
- Don't fight the Fed.
- Santa Claus rally.
- Sell in May and go away.

The wise investor takes each of these axioms' grain of truth with a grain of salt.

One way to combat the negative effects of framing is to develop a counterframe of your own. Benjamin Graham described the idea of imagining that you own a business in partnership with someone named Mr. Market. Mr. Market is a manic-depressive who is constantly quoting prices at which he will buy your share of the business or sell you his. You are free to ignore Mr. Market or take advantage of his excessive optimism or pessimism, but you should not fall under his spell and adopt his perspective; you should maintain your own.[4]

SOLUTION SUMMARY

1. **Use checklists.** Ensure that all relevant due diligence questions have been asked and nothing has been overlooked that sits outside the frame. Use a template that you develop rather than accepting the one that is offered by an interested party.
2. **Get a second opinion from a third party.** For consequential advice with a heavy technical component—such as that from doctors, lawyers, car mechanics, and building inspectors—be sure to get input from more than one expert, ideally a disinterested individual who does not stand to benefit from any transaction.
3. **Be wary of clichés and axioms.** Pithy sayings are memorable and often useful but not always applicable. Avoid oversimplifying complex problems. Look for nuance.

Chapter Seven

MENTAL ACCOUNTING

I will keep Social Security in a lockbox.

—Al Gore, former US vice president

Almost all decisions based on cost accounting are utterly wrong.

—Eliyahu Goldratt, businessman

AS THE ELEVATOR doors inside the Venetian Resort Las Vegas opened, Gabe exited and took several steps onto the casino floor before pausing to absorb the sensory overload of flashing lights, dinging bells, whooping and hollering of small celebrations, and live music from the nearby bar. He was fresh from his short flight from San Diego and knew that in a little under forty-eight hours, when it was time to depart, he would likely be sleep-deprived and spent of both energy and money.

His first stop was the blackjack table, where his friends Dave and Kevin were already midway through a six-deck shoe. Gabe sat down, pulled out five crisp Benjamin Franklins from his pocket, and slid them across the table. Without a word, the dealer gathered up the paper bills and returned the equivalent value of green $25 casino chips.

Over the next several hours, hands were dealt, shoes were shuffled, dealers were occasionally relieved, and the pile of composite clay chips on the red felt in front of Gabe gradually grew. With his success, the size of Gabe's bets grew from $25 per hand to $50, and then $75. The dealer began paying Gabe with black $100 chips by making change from the green $25 chips that he had bet. He resisted the urge to begin betting the $100 chips; instead, he decided to slip five black chips representing his original stake in his pocket. "Now I'm playing with the house's money," he said to his two friends, who were also winning.

With his initial bankroll intact, and aided by regular Jack-and-Coke deliveries, Gabe felt loose and allowed his bet size to continue to grow. His bankroll climbed to $4,000, but as the night wore on, his luck reversed and the pile of chips began to dwindle. By 3 A.M., he placed his last few chips in the betting circle and lost his last hand for the night.

You may recognize that throughout the evening, Gabe was engaged in mental accounting. He treated black chips differently from four green chips. He treated his initial stake as different from his winnings (i.e., "the house's money"). And he used his physical pants pocket as a separate deposit "account" to impose self-control.

Many of us attempt to bring order to an otherwise chaotic world by sorting and labeling things. Everything has its place. When we do this with money, it can lead to irrational decisions.

Money is said to have three purposes. It is (1) a store of value, (2) a unit of account, and (3) a medium of exchange. This third use, medium of exchange, stems from its fungibility. In a barter system, the apple farmer may need a pair of shoes, but the cobbler does not want apples. They must find a third, fungible commodity that they both value (historically, often gold or silver) to consummate their transaction.

Mental accounting takes this fungibility virtue and undermines it by dividing money into buckets that can be used only for specific purposes. Mental accounting is prevalent in our daily lives. Here are a few examples:

- A $100 cash birthday present is spent rather than saved because it was "meant to be used as a gift."
- An unexpected income tax refund is put into the vacation fund because it is "found money."
- A $2,500 credit card balance is allowed to roll over at an 18 percent annual percentage rate (APR), even though there is $5,000 in the savings account, because that's the "rainy day" money.
- The federal government earmarks $100 million to a particular state, with the mandate that it be used for the purpose of improving its schools. The politicians in that state elect to adjust the state budget so the $100 million that they had already been planning to use for schools will now be spent on another priority.

A former colleague who had previously worked at the headquarters of a savings and loan institution told me an amusing story that illustrated the concept of mental accounting. One day, one of their branches was robbed and money was stolen. One of the customers, an elderly woman, heard the news and made her way to the branch to speak to the manager. She asked, "They didn't get *my* money, did they?" In her mind, there were separate piles of money in the vault, each with the name of its respective accountholder.

At a cocktail party for parents of high school seniors, another father asked me a question with which he was wrestling related to his son's 529 college savings plan. He had originally elected a target date fund that had steadily shifted the account balance into conservative investments. He pointed out that the conservative investments were yielding only 4 percent, and it would be five years before his son would complete college, so shouldn't he take more risk? I asked him if he had other funds outside the 529 plan that could fill the gap if the 529 plan assets fell in value. He said that he did. Hearing that, I agreed with him that his instinct to take a bit more risk was probably correct, and I suggested that he think about the sources of college funding holistically, rather than in buckets with labels.

Mental accounting comes up in sports. Pundits will often label a game "must win," even early in a new season. Except in cases where a loss would entail playoff elimination, no game is literally "must win." The perceived importance of a game affects whether the team "gets up for it." Professional sports bettors often favor the team in a "revenge spot."

Mental accounting is a form of framing that can have positive as well as negative effects. For example, if you treat 401(k) savings as off limits because it is meant for retirement, that may be useful. However, if you frivolously spend money that you would otherwise save simply because of how you have labeled it, then mental accounting may be working against you.

Richard Thaler argued that the cognitive bias of loss aversion is at work with mental accounting.[1] *Loss aversion* is the idea that humans generally experience losses more intensely than equivalent gains. Also, a series of losses (i.e., "death by a thousand cuts") can be more painful than a single, large loss. As such, bucketing losses or spending into a single mental account can reduce the psychological hit.

Thaler also discussed the opening and closing of mental accounts. In investing, the account could be as narrowly defined as a single position in a stock (rather than the whole investment account). If funds need to be raised for a particular purpose, a position with an unrealized gain is more likely to be liquidated than one with an unrealized loss, which in mental accounting terms would imply "closing the account in the red." For taxable investors, this will mean paying capital gains tax on the gain.

I cringed one time I heard a portfolio manager describe the unrealized gain on one of his positions as "playing with the house's money." He seemed to be thinking of investing as a form of gambling and was using this mental accounting to justify holding onto a position that he would not otherwise buy fresh. I thought to myself, "That is not the 'house's money,' it's your clients' money."

The exercise of performing a zero-based rebuild of the entire portfolio, starting with a blank sheet of paper, can be an antidote to mental accounting. All positions are new and there are no winners and no losers, just fresh holdings looking forward from today. If you would not buy that stock for a hypothetical newly incepted portfolio, it is probably time to sell it in the real portfolio.

The zero-based rebuild is a form of reframing the topic to provide an alternative perspective. Another way of reframing is to take the mental accounts and aggregate them into a single balance sheet. On one side of the ledger are all the asset accounts. On the other side are the liability accounts. Assets represent each individual investment position, the house, the car, the savings account, and the 401(k), while the liabilities might be the student loan, the credit card balance, and the mortgage. Now, as an economist would say, compare use of the most marginal asset to the most marginal liability. If you have a savings account earning only 1 percent interest and a credit card balance charging 18 percent interest, then use the savings to pay the credit card bill.[2]

Mental accounting is not all bad. For certain people, putting income and spending, or assets and liabilities, into different buckets may impose a measure of self-discipline. For example, individuals may voluntarily elect to have more taxes than necessary withheld from their paycheck, allowing the excess to accumulate into a refund, which they then put into savings. They do this because they know that otherwise, they would spend the extra money each week. A classical economist would view this behavior as suboptimal, though, arguing that tax refunds should not be celebrated since they effectively represent an interest-free loan to the government, but for those who lack self-discipline, it may be the least-bad practical option.

Another reason not to look down on mental accounting is if the character and rules of the accounts truly differ in some important respect. For example, money in an individual retirement account (IRA) differs not only because it is labeled "retirement money," but because early withdrawal usually comes with penalties and tax obligations. Likewise, paying down a mortgage may not be the best use of funds since the interest on a mortgage is often tax deductible.

Richard Thaler and Cass Sunstein have promoted the idea that individuals can be "nudged" into certain desirable behaviors by governments and employers.[3] An example of this involves employer-sponsored retirement plans like 401(k)s. When new employees join a company, they are more likely to enroll in the plan and build retirement savings if the default is to opt in rather than opt out. In either case, the employees can do something different, but the default setting benefits from inertia.

SOLUTION SUMMARY

1. **Reframe your mental accounts.** Aggregate all assets and liabilities. Likewise, aggregate all income and spending. Against your comprehensive balance sheet and income statement, consider the highest and best use of an incremental dollar.
2. **Avoid labels.** Naming assets "a rainy day fund" or "the house's money" may lead to inconsistent decisions.
3. **If you can't beat 'em, join 'em.** Use "nudge" concepts to enforce self-discipline. For example, take advantage of mental accounting's positive effects by increasing payroll deductions to favor saving over spending.

Chapter Eight

ANCHORING

To reach a port, we must sail—sail, not tie at anchor—sail, not drift.

—Franklin D. Roosevelt, 32nd US president

Have an anchor so that life doesn't toss you around.

—Debby Ryan, actress

ON DECEMBER 11, 2000, Alex Rodriguez ("A-Rod"), shortstop for the Seattle Mariners, signed a ten-year, $252 million contract to play for the Texas Rangers. At the time, it was the largest baseball contract ever signed, more than double the prior record. Although A-Rod played well for the Rangers, the team lost more than half of their games and struggled under the weight of his contract. After three years, he was traded to the New York Yankees. Despite the contract generally being regarded as too expensive, it had the effect of permanently resetting the market for star baseball players. Other players, their agents, and team owners all anchored to this bellwether contract.

Daniel Kahneman and Amos Tversky identified "anchoring and adjustment" in 1974. In their experiment, a wheel with numbers from 1–100 was spun and rigged to land on either the number 10 or 65. Each subject was separately asked to guess whether the percentage of countries in the United Nations that were African was above or below that number, followed by a guess of the actual percentage. Those who anchored to the higher number tended to guess a greater percentage.[1]

Anchoring, sometimes referred to as "focalism," occurs when one piece of information is given excessive or exclusive weight in the decision-making process. This typically occurs because the piece of information is one of the first received (i.e., the primacy effect) or because it is particularly dramatic or vivid, and therefore easy to recall.

The primacy effect leads to anchoring. The first pieces of information that we receive on a topic take on greater importance and are given more weight in the decision-making process. Even as new information comes in, some of which may contradict the initial data, we find it difficult to let go of the anchor.

Being willing to incorporate new information versus dogmatically sticking to an initial point of view is what statisticians refer to as "updating one's priors." The Bayesian approach to statistics blends new information with prior knowledge.

Anchoring is commonplace in the investment business. Share prices, earnings estimates, valuation models, and other metrics can all serve as anchors. These anchors can be helpful if they are used to establish a baseline from which to judge new information as it arrives, but they also can cause damage if they become an inflexible crutch or excuse for dismissing red flags.

Equity investors often anchor to a narrower range of potential outcomes than is warranted. A common tool used in corporate finance for the purposes of valuing a financial asset or investment such as a company, piece of real estate, or new product is a discounted cash flow (DCF) model. The basic idea is to project several years of cash flows and then use a discounted rate of interest to calculate their net present value. For assets that are perpetuities (such as a share of common stock in a public company), the residual value beyond the immediate forecast horizon is dealt with by assuming a steady-state growth rate. The DCF has the advantages of being precise and theoretically accurate. If you plug in the correct assumptions, you get a mathematically accurate answer. Despite these obvious benefits, many professional investors eschew DCF analysis.

One of the complaints of DCF skeptics is that the output is highly sensitive to the chosen discount rate and perpetuity growth rate. In my opinion, this is a feature, not a bug. One only needs to observe the volatility of the typical stock over the course of a year to understand that the market's debate over the fair value of a particular company covers a wide range.

To obtain a narrower range of forecast values, many investors favor multiples-based approaches, such as the use of price-to-earnings (P/E) ratios or enterprise value/earnings before interest, taxes, depreciation, and amortization (EV/EBITDA) multiples. In this case, the investor must merely forecast the denominator, such as earnings per share (EPS), and then apply an appropriate multiple to those earnings. For example, if a company is forecast to earn $2 per share in the following twelve months, and the analyst deems 15 to be the right multiple, the stock is seen to be worth $30 per share. The analyst might develop a range of potential scenarios by varying the EPS estimates up and down by 10 percent and varying the multiple up and down by 2 points. In this case, the valuation range for the stock would be a low of $23.40 (13 × $1.80) to a high of $37.40 (17 × $2.20).

Two former colleagues at Eaton Vance conducted a study to understand how much reported EPS differed from the consensus market estimate from one year prior. They discovered a staggering 43 percent average variance. So, with a P/E-based approach, the typical investor is likely not considering a wide enough range of potential outcomes.

In pursuit of a valuation methodology that is less sensitive to chosen inputs, the P/E investors have merely succeeded in blinding themselves to the naturally occurring variance and ruling out plausible scenarios. On several occasions when debating the merits of DCFs with junior equity analysts, I have put them through a version of the following thought experiment: Suppose that you have access to a time machine and go back to January 1, 2003. What P/E multiple would you put on the shares of Amazon? Most people would recognize that for a company with such a bright future at that time, a very high multiple would be warranted. But is the right figure 50x, 75x, 100x, or something else?

To answer with the benefit of hindsight, start with the fact that Amazon shares closed 2024 at a price of $219. Next, pick a compound annual rate of return that would have been satisfactory for this investment; I will use 10 percent, the long-term historical return on US stocks.[2] To generate a final investment value of $219 at a 10 percent annual rate of return over the twenty-two-year period beginning on January 1, 2003, the initial investment value would have been $26.90. The actual price of Amazon shares at that time was approximately 94 cents (adjusted for subsequent stock splits). In other words, if early 2003 investors had known what was to come, they would have paid more than twenty-eight times the prevailing price. Amazon earned $0.0045 (approximately half a penny) in 2003, so the prevailing P/E ratio was a seemingly nosebleed level of

209x. With the benefit of perfect foresight, the "correct" P/E multiple would have been 5,978x at that time.

The lesson from the preceding valuation example is not that it is all right to ignore valuation metrics. Rather, it is to argue that anchoring to familiar or comfortable rules of thumb can lead one astray, particularly when dealing with outliers like Amazon.

It is not only investors who anchor to certain metrics when making corporate valuation judgments. Boards of directors do too. When a company is considering selling itself to a potential suitor, its board of directors obviously wants the highest price possible. Typically, an acquirer must pay a premium, perhaps 15–30 percent, to entice the target company to agree to sell. In cases where the target company's share price is meaningfully below its fifty-two-week high, it can be difficult to consummate a transaction. For example, imagine a hypothetical company whose shares were trading at $150 just six months ago, but due to an economic downturn and a couple of company-specific issues, the shares today are priced at $100. A competitor, perhaps eyeing the attractive price, comes along and offers a 40 percent premium: $140 per share. Many corporate board directors will be reluctant to agree to this price since it does not get them back to the $150 that is still fresh in their memories. Interestingly, once a year has passed and the recollection of the $150 price fades, that reference price will represent less of an anchor.

A close cousin of the anchoring effect is *conservatism bias*, which results from insufficient adjustment to new data. It occurs when new, potentially disconfirming information is not given enough weight. An example of this can be found in the world of professional sports betting. The most successful, winning sports bettors often work with data scientists to write the code to build sophisticated prediction models. At the start of a new season, the model builder (known as the "originator") relies on data from the prior season, along with adjustments for personnel changes during the offseason. As the new season unfolds, a decision must be made. How much should the new data be weighed versus priors? If the new data is overemphasized, the model builder risks overreacting to small datasets. If the new data is given insufficient weight, then this conservatism bias may delay the recognition of an important change that has occurred, rendering the model's output inaccurate.

In financial markets, momentum is a quantitative statistical factor that has proved highly profitable across asset classes. *Momentum* is the idea that once the price of a stock, bond, commodity, or other financial instrument increases, it will tend to continue to rise or outperform other assets. This suggests that investors tend to underreact to new information, a display of conservatism bias at work.

Countering the anchoring effect is tricky because it can be useful in moderation. Having a baseline understanding of a situation and not reacting to every tidbit of new information that arrives can serve a purpose. The problem arises when stubborn adherence to the anchor holds one back from seeing that things have changed and now the old rule of thumb or understanding is invalid.

Since anchoring works by overemphasizing an early or vivid piece of information and underweighting the steady drip of new data, one needs to break the cycle by finding a way to step back and create discontinuity in the analysis. There are several ways to do this.

A colleague acting as devil's advocate can be helpful. If a second person looks independently at the same decision, he or she may not anchor to the same preconception or baseline. For the devil's advocate approach to be effective, it is best that they work independent of the proponent of the thesis or idea. Ideally, the devil's advocate believes in the counterargument rather than simply going through the motions of building a surface-level strawman to be knocked down easily.

A leader at Goldman Sachs regularly instructed the team to "embrace uncertainty." It is human nature to feel anxiety. As value investors, stocks with "overhangs," "hair," or other forms of blemishes can become mispriced, and a willingness to accept those uncertainties can be rewarding.

SOLUTION SUMMARY

1. **Use the full toolbox.** When valuing an investment security, use several approaches and metrics. If they produce meaningfully different answers, dig into understanding why. Select the metric or metrics that best capture the thesis and expectations rather than blindly taking a simple average.
2. **Appoint a devil's advocate.** Among their other responsibilities, devil's advocates should take it upon themselves to identify any anchoring or unquestioned assumptions that are informing your decision.
3. **Embrace uncertainty.** Resist the urge to narrow the range of potential outcomes. Accept that the future is unknowable.

Chapter Nine

RECENCY BIAS

Don't fight the tape.
—Marty Zweig, Wall Street strategist

Never fight the last war.
—Miyamoto Musashi, seventeenth-century Japanese swordsman

AT 8 P.M. CENTRAL STANDARD TIME on June 3, 1992, the Chicago Bulls stepped onto the court in the old Chicago Stadium to face the Portland Trail Blazers in game 1 of the 1992 NBA Championship Finals. For most of the season, and increasingly as the playoffs unfolded, the national media had hyped the rivalry of Michael Jordan and Clyde Drexler. *Sports Illustrated* went as far as labeling Drexler as Jordan's number 1 rival. No doubt, Jordan felt that he had something to prove as he stepped onto the floor that evening. Over the ensuing twenty-four minutes of game time, Jordan played arguably the best half of playoff basketball in history. He scored a record thirty-five points and made six three-point shots. After the last of these three-pointers, Jordan famously turned to the television announcer's table where Magic Johnson sat, shook his head slowly, and shrugged, as if to say, "I don't know how I am doing this either." This iconic image became known as "The Shrug."

Along with 12.4 million other households, I was privileged to watch this game live on television. It was seemingly clear to all who were watching that Jordan "could do no wrong," "was in the zone," and "had the hot hand." After the game, Jordan himself said, "Next thing you know, shots started dropping from everywhere . . . I started running for the 3-point line. It felt like a free throw, really."[1]

And yet there has been a four-decade debate among researchers as to whether there is such a thing as streaky athletic performance that is not explained by randomness and chance. This theory is known as "the hot-hand fallacy."[2]

The hot-hand fallacy argues that observers overemphasize recent performance, which is nothing more than statistical noise. It is the functional opposite of the gambler's fallacy. Whereas the gambler's fallacy results from a gambler's belief that an outcome of an event (such as the roll of a die or toss of a coin) is "due" since it has not occurred in the recent past, believers in the hot-hand fallacy argue that a short streak is likely to continue or repeat itself in the future. In both cases, the sample sizes are too small, and the advocate for the theory is falling victim to the "small number problem." In other words, the baseline statistic (e.g., a particular basketball player's shooting percentage or the 50 percent probability of a coin flip resulting in tails) should be emphasized, and temporary deviation from the norm should be ignored.

The hot-hand fallacy and the gambler's fallacy are both examples of recency bias. *Recency bias* occurs when recent events are given too much weight, while events from a larger, older sample are ignored or deemphasized.

Speaking of recency, a more recent example of the hot hand in action can be found in the men's basketball gold medal game in the 2024 Summer Olympics. In this game, the United States faced France. The game was close until the final three minutes, when US guard Steph Curry shot four increasingly audacious three-point shots, making each of them. In an interview on *Hot Ones* twelve months prior to the Olympics, Curry had been asked about the research suggesting that the concept of the hot hand does not exist, and he replied that the authors "don't know what they're talking about at all." On another occasion, he said, "It's literally a tangible, physical sensation of all I need is to get this ball off my fingertips and it's going to go in."[3]

Although the concept of the hot-hand fallacy fits neatly into this chapter on recency bias, the theory has come under criticism in recent years, and not just by ball players and armchair sports fans. In 2018, two researchers discovered a slight bias in the selection criteria for the data in the original study.[4] Once this was corrected, a modest hot-hand effect could be detected in the data. Others found that in the National Basketball Association (NBA), players tend to take more difficult shots following a series of successfully made ones, thus rendering the assumption of independent trials incorrect.[5]

I believe that there is such a thing as a "flow state" or "zone" where an athlete (or thinker) can perform at an elevated level due to a combination of confidence and focus, but this is rare. In investment markets, there is a documented momentum effect of which quantitative investors have been able to take advantage. For nonquants, extrapolation should be used with caution.

Recency bias is related to the "serial position effect," first documented by German psychologist Hermann Ebbinghaus in the late 1800s.[6] Ebbinghaus discovered that when he gave subjects a list of words, they were more likely to later recall those words that were placed near the beginning or end of the list. Those words in the middle were the most difficult for people to remember. He called the ability to remember words early in the list the "primacy effect," and the ability to name those words at the end of the list the "recency effect." The recency effect is also tied to the *availability heuristic*, where the human mind tends to use information that is easily recalled when making decisions.

In 1966, Henry Glanzer and Anita Cunitz conducted experiments to further develop the theory of serial position effect.[7] They concluded that the primacy effect was the result of storing information in the brain's long-term memory, while the recency effect was tied to short-term memory.

For professional investors, recency bias is a real problem. Days or weeks will go by with very little fresh news or information on a company or its industry. Then, all of a sudden, there will be an event or announcement of some sort. Perhaps a new product launch, a lawsuit, a management change, or an earnings report with surprising news. Inevitably, this will cause a short-term burst of volatility, with the stock price gapping up or down as investors wrestle with the relative importance of this new information and attempt to price it in. Earlier, we looked at how bias can lead to investors being dismissive of new information, particularly if it is negative. Recency bias is the opposite problem. Instead of ignoring a new piece of information, we place too much emphasis on it and overreact.

An investment leader colleague developed a portfolio exercise to combat recency bias. Periodically, he would ask the members of his investment team to imagine that they worked as financial journalists with access to a time machine. They would transport themselves twelve months into the future and write the headline of the front page of the *Financial Times*. We had so much success with this tool that we engaged actual financial journalists at media luncheons to undertake the exercise. Inevitably, the submissions were funny and provocative. The primary benefit of doing this is that it extracts you from the noise of the current moment. It forces you to deemphasize recent news that may not be long-lasting and to imagine what might come to pass. It leads one to consider seasonality, dates on the calendar, and potential news flow. Is an election coming up? Is there a current element of uncertainty that the market is pricing in, which will have dissipated within a year?

As a contrarian running against the herd, I like to invest in companies with so-called headline risk because the headlines in question have usually occurred in the recent past, causing excessive fear and providing an attractive entry point. Warren Buffett has said, "You pay a high price in the stock market for a cheery consensus." The corollary is also true: You pay a low price in the stock market when there is headline risk.

One benefit of looking at the future as if it has already occurred is that it is subtly different from forecasting. Most forecasts are anchored to the current moment or current trend line. By leaping forward in time and looking back, one becomes less tethered to preconceptions. A wider range of possibilities can be examined. Nonlinear outcomes and discontinuous data series become more feasible.

I have come to believe that the best way to invest is to get out of the forecasting business altogether. At least, get out of the business of attempting to forecast with pinpoint accuracy. Many professional investors reject this view and prefer to make detailed forecasts.

The specific forecast to which most investors pay the closest attention is the quarterly earnings per share (EPS). Every ninety days or so, public companies put out a press release summarizing their results for the quarter. Most companies host an earnings conference call later that same day to have the company's CEO, chief financial officer (CFO), and (sometimes) other members of senior management discuss the results and field questions. These earnings releases are typically made outside market hours. When the stock market reopens later that morning (or the next morning, if the release comes out in the late afternoon), the company's stock price will often gap up or down and trade with more volatility than is typical.

As investors and Wall Street sell-side analysts scour the press release and put out notes with initial reactions, their headlines typically focus on whether the EPS figure beat the company's prior guidance or published consensus EPS estimates of the sell-side analysts themselves. If the company not only beats the EPS guidance but raises forward-looking guidance, then backers of the company's stock will proudly tout that it was a "beat-and-raise quarter." I hate this phrase.

The headline of having beaten an EPS estimate provides minimal information in and of itself. There are several reasons for this. First, the reported earnings results can be manipulated in multiple legal ways. Various accounting assumptions go into a company's financial statements. Revenue recognition policies, reserve builds and releases, bonus accruals, and share buybacks are just a few of the levers that CFOs can pull to produce a desired result in the short run. Second, companies are typically conservative with their earnings guidance, knowing that investors like positive surprises. Third, many companies monitor consensus earnings estimates, and if the company's results are running behind expectations midquarter, they will sometimes "talk down" numbers.[8]

The market has figured all of this out. The initial reaction of a company's stock price to an earnings beat is not nearly as predictable as it once was.

While a headline EPS "beat" carries minimal direct information, an EPS "miss" is an entirely different kettle of fish. If a company has gone through the process of setting low expectations, pulling accounting levers to hit those low expectations, and encouraging sell-side analysts to keep their forecasts in check—and *still* misses the number—something may be going wrong with the business. This is why I don't have much sympathy for a CEO who says, "We only missed by a penny; I don't understand why our stock is down 10 percent."

Warren Buffett does not bother with quarterly press releases or earnings calls for his company, Berkshire Hathaway. Rather, he allows the company's financial results to speak for themselves in the firm's 10-Q regulatory filings. He guides his investors to focus on longer-term business performance by writing a thoughtful annual shareholder letter with a balanced review of results, and a lengthy shareholder meeting, where he fields questions for several hours.

OK, fine, you may be tempted to say. But if forecasting a company's future profits is not the path to investing success, what is? I believe that the answer lies in allowing one's mind to entertain a wide range of future paths. Think in terms of a decision tree with nodes, each with a different probability that leads to a range of other outcomes. But even this is incomplete because it is finite in nature. In the early 2000s, I had the opportunity to hear a talk by Peter Bernstein, author of *Against the Gods: The Remarkable Story of Risk*, who was considered one of the leading experts on the topic of risk. He made the point that when one adds up the nodes on a decision tree, it always sums to 100 percent. "But what about all the possibilities that you didn't even think of?" So even the tool of a decision tree falls short by attempting to bring a finite order to the inherent uncertainty of the future. Author and former derivatives trader Nassim Taleb referred to these unseen possibilities as "black swans," and US Secretary of Defense Donald Rumsfeld called them "unknown unknowns."

As investors, we need to be aware that many more things can happen than will happen.[9] Embrace the uncertainty.

SOLUTION SUMMARY

1. **Be a time traveler.** Write the newspaper headline for one year hence. Look at today from the perspective of the future. Which of today's concerns will still be present in a year?

(*continued on next page*)

(*continued from previous page*)

2. **Test against your priors.** Review new information in the context of your model or other documentation. If they are in conflict, gather more data and take time to reflect on whether the new information should be emphasized or downplayed.
3. **Make use of the multiverse.** Think in terms of decision trees and a range of outcomes, each with its own probability, rather than a single, pinpoint forecast.

Chapter Ten

SHORT-TERMISM

Perfection of character is this: To live each day as if it were your last, without frenzy, without apathy, without pretense.

—Marcus Aurelius, second-century Roman emperor

If you live each day as if it were your last, you will be walking around in dirty clothes all the time. Who is going to do laundry on the last day of their life?

—Unknown comedian

ONE OF AESOP'S best-known fables is *The Ant and the Grasshopper*:[1]

In a field one summer's day a Grasshopper was hopping about, chirping and singing to its heart's content. An Ant passed by, bearing along with great toil an ear of corn he was taking to the nest.

"Why not come and chat with me," said the Grasshopper, "instead of toiling and moiling in that way?"

"I am helping to lay up food for the winter," said the Ant, "and recommend you to do the same."

"Why bother about winter?" said the Grasshopper; "we have got plenty of food at present." But the Ant went on its way and continued its toil.

When the winter came the Grasshopper had no food and found itself dying of hunger, while it saw the ants distributing every day corn and grain from the stores they had collected in the summer. Then the Grasshopper knew:

It is best to prepare for the days of necessity.

The choice between instant and delayed gratification is one that humans face every day throughout our lives. Society generally looks favorably on those who delay their gratification. Those who repeatedly opt for instant gratification without regard for the future are said to be guilty of *short-termism*.

In finance, the evaluation of the present versus the future is a bedrock principle known as the *time value of money*. Everything else follows this iron law. Whether it is valuing a business, deciding whether to build a factory, considering an acquisition or, on the personal level, deciding how much of your salary to put away each month for retirement, the decision is undergirded by the idea that money has differing values through time.

If you had the choice between having a dollar today or a dollar one year from now, you would always choose a dollar today. A dollar today must be worth at least that of a dollar in the future because if it were worth less, you could always take today's dollar and simply stuff it under your mattress or put it in a cookie jar and wait for time to elapse.[2] If you were offered two dollars in one year versus one dollar today, you would be wise to be patient and wait for the larger amount. Somewhere between one dollar and two dollars lies the amount of money where you would be indifferent between a dollar today and that alternative amount one year hence. The percentage difference between those two numbers is known as the *discount rate* of interest.

For example, if your tipping point is $1.05 one year from now versus $1 today, then your discount rate is 5 percent.

The discount rate can vary from person to person depending on their individual preferences between consumption today and consumption in the future. It can also vary based on the level of expected inflation over the next twelve months (or whatever period is being priced). Another influence on the discount rate is the level of certainty that the payment will be made in the future, either because the counterparty's creditworthiness is in question or because the amount to be received is variable, such as with the cash flows that a company generates for its shareholders.

I once attended a meeting with the provocative title, "How Time Value of Money Explains Why Socialism Can Never Work." The lecturer argued that in the absence of the private ownership of capital and the right to earn a profit from that capital investment, there would be no incentive to save or take a long-term perspective. Everyone would eat their seed corn.

Martín de Azpilcueta, a sixteenth-century Spanish economist and religious scholar, is credited with first conceptualizing the time value of money. He argued that money exchange is not unnatural, as it simply puts money on the same level as any other merchandise.[3]

The concept of short-termism relates to the time value of money, in that it implies a high preference for current consumption over long-term savings and investment. In other words, the implied discount rate is very high if short-termism exists.

The concept of discount rates exists beyond financial markets. For example, by observing National Football League

(NFL) draft trades, economists Cade Massey and Richard Thaler were able to calculate discount rates for the value of draft picks across time.[4] The rule of thumb that NFL general managers (GMs) use is that one round of draft position is worth one year of delay. In other words, a third-round pick from the current draft is worth a second-round pick in next year's draft. By Massey and Thaler's calculations, this works out to a staggering annual discount rate of 136 percent! This level of short-termism likely undermines a team's ability to win in the long run, although it is somewhat understandable given the short tenure of most NFL GMs.

The scholarly research on the topic of short-termism is relatively recent and inconclusive. It has typically centered around corporate decisions and executive management incentives, particularly in the United States. The research is mixed on the question of whether financial markets reward companies for long-term decisions.[5]

I have observed that companies that truly think and act for the long term, such as Amazon and Berkshire Hathaway, are given the benefit of the doubt by investors. Over the years, sell-side analysts have repeatedly called for Amazon to allow more of its revenue to fall to the bottom line, only to be disappointed by the company's decisions to increase expenses in pro-growth initiatives or new ventures. Inevitably, this long-term thinking has been rewarded in the company's stock price, as investors focus on pro forma or potential profit margins and find ways to value the company by giving it credit for this value-added spending.

Many public company CEOs and chief financial officers (CFOs) complain that the market is too short-term oriented when they report a quarterly result that comes up a penny short. However, if the "miss" is accompanied by underlying trends that say something negative about the long-term health of the company and its returns on capital or growth potential, then a negative reaction is warranted, particularly by long-term investors.

My advice to public company CEOs and CFOs is this: You get the investor base that you deserve. If you condition your investors to expect steady quarterly results with regular earnings "beats," then you will be punished when you miss. If you are clear with investors that your decisions are based on maximizing the long-term intrinsic value per share of your company's stock, and you demonstrate it with your actions, then you will attract a more patient investor base.

Warren Buffett once said, "I buy on the assumption that they could close the market the next day and not reopen it for five years." To encourage this mode of thinking, I designed a portfolio exercise, which I dubbed "Robinson Crusoe." Upon relocating to Goldman Sach's London office in the spring of 2008, I found myself working with several new colleagues who had a strong value approach to investing. Although I consider myself a value investor, the approach of screening for low price-to-earnings (P/E) stocks did not suit the times. It inevitably led one to favor cyclical or heavily indebted companies during an unfolding global financial crisis.

I wanted the investment team to identify companies that would be long-term winners regardless of the economic backdrop. Along with a colleague, I had developed something that we called "the list," which included the small handful of companies that compounded value over long periods of time. They could be bought once and held forever. One hallmark of the list was that if you had had the unfortunate timing of always buying the stock at its fifty-two-week high for each of the past ten years, you did not have to wait long to be back above water and your compound return on your investment was still excellent.

This is not to say that the entry-point valuation did not matter, but if you are looking to invest in the world's best businesses, valuation should be done late in the process rather than as an initial screen. Also, valuation work needs to go beyond simply slapping P/E multiples on twelve-month forward earnings per share (EPS) estimates. Several of the companies from the original "list" are given here.

The Original "List" of Long-Term Compounders

Amazon	EOG Resources
Amphenol	Graco
Berkshire Hathaway	Landstar
Costco	Markel
C. H. Robinson	M&T Bank
Disney	NVR Corp.

To encourage the search for these long-term winners in the European market, I ran the following portfolio exercise in the summer of 2008:

> Imagine that you are Robinson Crusoe, marooned on a desert island for the next five to seven years. You have no phone or other means of communication, so you cannot contact your

> broker to trade your position. Whatever was the last stock you purchased, you are stuck with it until you are rescued. For the purposes of this exercise, set valuation considerations to the side. Which one special company in your coverage universe has the competitive moat, high returns on invested capital, and future runway such that when you are rescued in five to seven years, you are confident that the business will be larger, stronger, and more valuable than it is today?

We stopped calling it "the list" and began referring to these companies as "Robinson Crusoe" stocks. The original list of European "Robinson Crusoe" companies from 2008 is shown here.

"Robinson Crusoe" Companies in Europe

Admiral Group	Kerry Group
Assa Abloy	Lindt & Spruengli
Atlas Copco	Nestlé
Kuehne Nagel	Novo Nordisk

Going back a couple of years to 2006, when I was focused on potential investment ideas among publicly listed restaurant chains, the topic of short-termism came up. At that time, there were concerns among investors that the US economy had become saturated with casual dining restaurants that were largely indistinguishable from one another. Applebee's, Olive Garden, Chili's, Outback Steakhouse, Longhorn Steakhouse, Red Lobster, Ruby Tuesday, Cheesecake Factory . . . they all seemed to be about the same. The general rule of thumb in the restaurant industry is that you need year-over-year growth in same-store sales (i.e., ignoring growth from opening new locations) of about 2 percent to maintain current profit margin levels. Many restaurants were experiencing weak foot traffic and having trouble hitting this 2 percent figure. There were also increases in food supply costs that further pressured profit margins.

Against this difficult industry backdrop, the question seemingly coming from every Wall Street analyst's lips was, "What plan do you have to reduce your expenses and maintain your profit margin?" Such was the obsession with maintaining a smooth profit trajectory and removing any cyclicality from the earnings stream.

I vividly recall a meeting that I had around this time with the CEO of Texas Roadhouse, one of those seemingly undistinguished casual dining places. At one point in the conversation, I asked the generic question about plans for cost cutting. The answer that I received was so unexpected and thoughtful that I remember it two decades later:

> Look, Eddie, there are lots of things we could do to cut costs. We could use frozen chicken instead of fresh chicken. We could take a few French fries off your plate. We could cut back on payroll by taking a member of the waitstaff out of the restaurant. At first, you would not notice a difference. But then, six months later, you would say to yourself, "Texas Roadhouse . . . I used to love that place but it's just not the same anymore and I can't quite say why."

It is not surprising to me that the stock price of Texas Roadhouse has been a ten-bagger since the day of that meeting.[6] Taking a long-term perspective to maintain a consistent customer experience is the heart of building brand loyalty. In recent times, when inflationary pressures have been high across the economy, many investment analysts have asked company managements some version of the question, "Are you able to pass those costs along to your customers?" It is the rare, truly long-term investor who would think to ask, "Even if your customers can bear a price increase, should you consider absorbing some or all of the cost pressure into your own short-term profit margin to maintain the loyalty and expectations of your customers?" Costco offers an example of this enlightened thinking by maintaining a stable price of $4.99 on rotisserie chicken during short-term spikes in poultry prices, even though they take a loss on every chicken sold at those times, because they know that for many of their customers, the chicken was what brought them into the store.

One of the rewarding aspects of working as a professional investor is the unstructured nature of one's day. Each day is different. One can come into the office in the morning and find oneself working on something completely unexpected by the afternoon. I suppose that it is a bit like working in a newsroom. With that lack of structure comes the risk of being distracted and focusing only on what is immediately in front of you, not finding the time to get to longer-term projects. An investment analyst's time is often dictated by items on the calendar such as scheduled earnings releases, corporate investor days, investment conferences, and whichever CEOs happen to be in town that week making the rounds and meeting with investors on non-deal road shows. Each of these events requires preparation and reflection before and after the event. One year, as things wound down in December, I realized that there were several companies that I was interested in but upon which I had not gotten around to doing the deep work. To regain control of my time, I sent an e-mail to half a dozen equity research salespeople who covered me as a client:

> As the year ends, I want to thank you for your efforts in supporting me and my firm. In the first six months of the new year, I intend to be purposeful with my time. I will be focusing on the following companies: *[A, B, C, X, Y, Z]*. If you are hosting the management teams of these companies for investor meetings, please think of me. If your analyst writes something particularly insightful about these companies, please forward it to me.

Since I was known as someone who did not spend much time "talking to the Street" or returning phone calls from salespeople, they appreciated the recognition and direction that I gave them.

Later, we decided to turn this concept of taking back one's time by setting deadlines into a portfolio exercise called "Six for Six." Each member of the team would be asked to identify six stocks that they planned to do a deep level of work on during the next six months. By committing to this list and this deadline, with an expectation that they would report back to the group as they completed their work, we were able to resist the default urge to react to short-term news flows.

SOLUTION SUMMARY

1. **Use a discount rate to price the future.** Think in terms of the trade-offs between sacrifices made today and benefits to be derived tomorrow.
2. **Act like Robinson Crusoe.** Imagine that you have a single decision to make and must live with the outcome of that decision, but also that you have the freedom of a long period of time before the decision will be evaluated.
3. **Set a deadline.** For medium- to long-term projects, write down milestones and completion dates and hold yourself accountable for them.

Chapter Eleven

CONFIRMATION BIAS

There are always going to be skeptics. Prove them wrong.
—Robert Kiyosaki, author of *Rich Dad Poor Dad*

Constantly think about how you could be doing things better and questioning yourself.
—Elon Musk, entrepreneur and investor

IMAGINE THAT you are the parent of kids who have been begging you for a family pet. After contemplating the idea for a few months, you relent. The decision is between a dog and a cat. You open your internet browser and head over to Google to do a bit of research. You type in, "Are dogs better than cats?"

At the top of the page of results is an article from thesprucepets.com titled "10 Reasons Dogs Are Better Than Cats." The article opens with the line, "In many people's opinion, dogs are better than cats. Dogs are more trainable, use the bathroom outside, can protect you, and promote a more active lifestyle. Having a dog has many benefits that make it better than having a cat."

Meanwhile, Vanessa, one of your friends who lives alone, has been thinking about getting a pet as a companion. She does her own search, asking Google the question, "Are cats better than dogs?"

At the top of the page of your friend's results is an article from freshpet.com titled "10 Reasons Why Cats Make Great Pets." The article argues that compared to dogs, cats are quiet, low-maintenance, and easy to house-train, along with several other positive attributes.

You and your friend were seemingly undertaking the same project to research which type of pet to bring into your homes. Yet the answers you received to your similar questions were opposites of one another. How is this possible? The answer: You each engaged in confirmation bias in how you phrased your queries.[1] It is also likely that your browsing history tipped off Google's algorithms to your respective preferences, reinforcing your subconscious leanings.

Confirmation bias is the tendency to search for, interpret, favor, and recall information in a way that confirms or supports one's prior beliefs or values. People display this bias when they select information that supports their views, ignoring contrary information, or when they interpret ambiguous evidence as supporting their existing attitudes. The effect is strongest for desired outcomes, emotionally charged issues, and deeply entrenched beliefs."[2] One of the reasons that confirmation bias is so difficult to overcome is that it is sneaky and hard to spot.

Peter Wason, an English psychologist, is generally credited with having first identified confirmation bias in 1960, when he conducted his ingenious 2-4-6 experiment. Wason administered his experiment to twenty-nine undergraduate students. Each subject was given the following instructions:[3]

> You will be given three numbers which conform to a simple rule that I have in mind. This rule is concerned with a relation between any three numbers and not with their absolute magnitude, i.e. it is not a rule like all numbers above (or below) 50, etc.
>
> Your aim is to discover this rule by writing down sets of three numbers, together with reasons for your choice of them. After you have written down each set, I shall tell you whether your numbers conform to the rule or not, and you can make a note of this outcome on the record sheet provided. There is no time limit but you should try to discover this rule by citing the minimum sets of numbers.
>
> Remember that your aim is not simply to find numbers which conform to the rule, but to discover the rule itself. When you feel highly confident that you have discovered it, and not before, you are to write it down and tell me what it is. Have you any questions?

The subject was then given the initial sequence of numbers, "2-4-6." Obviously, there are many rules that would fit this sequence of numbers. Examples include "increasing by 2," "only even numbers," and "a middle number that is the arithmetic mean of the other two." The simple rule that Wason had in mind was, "three numbers in increasing order of magnitude."

Of the twenty-nine subjects, only six generated the correct rule on their first announcement. Another ten got it on their second declaration, and eight of the subjects never discovered the rule at all. Wason was surprised by the poor performance of the subjects. The incorrect rule guesses typically fit the sequence of numbers that had been tested but were more specific than the general rule. For several of the students who guessed incorrectly, they generated a hypothesis and then tested only sequences of numbers consistent with that hypothesis. In certain cases, even after being informed that their hypothesis was incorrect, they simply reworded or mildly tweaked their theory and tried again. In other cases, they also continued to test sequences of numbers that were consistent with the old, disproven hypothesis. In other words, the subjects were searching for evidence to support their theories and neglected the basic but important step of attempting to falsify their hypotheses.

Investors should—like a good scientist—develop a hypothesis and then test it with experiments and data collection. In both cases, it is easy for the experiment to inadvertently be set up—or for the data to be interpreted—in a way that biases the outcome in favor of the hypothesis.

My rabbit ears would stick up whenever I heard one of our analysts say some version of, "I just got back from a meeting with the company management, and everything I heard confirmed my thesis on the stock." All I could think was, "Did you ask the right probing questions, or did you go into the meeting looking to prove yourself right?"

For a fundamental equity analyst, one of the ways in which due diligence is conducted on a portfolio holding or prospective new one is to regularly speak with the senior management of the company. These meetings can take many forms. The meeting could be held in the asset management firm's offices, as senior management teams regularly travel on "nondeal road shows" to meet with their shareholders and prospective investors. It could be held at the company's headquarters. Alternatively, the venue could be at a restaurant or an industry conference at a hotel sponsored by a Wall Street brokerage firm.

In these corporate access meetings, the other side of the table can include the CEO, chief financial officer (CFO), division head, director of investor relations, or any combination of these. On the investment analyst's side of the table, it could be the analyst on their own or in the company of colleagues, including portfolio managers who own the stock. If the meeting is outside the firm's own offices, they may be joined by analysts from competitor firms. The duration of this meeting can be as short as twenty-five minutes, or this can be a series of hour-long meetings with different individuals from the firm.

I estimate that over the course of my career, I have attended more than 2,500 of these investment due diligence meetings, sometimes as the lead interviewer, other times as an observer. I have found them to be the perfect petri dish for the culture of confirmation bias to grow.

These management meetings can be intimidating for the interviewer. On one side of the table might sit the CEO of a Fortune 500 company, wearing a well-tailored business suit, accompanied by several of their colleagues. On the other side of the table sit several colleagues, often including the analyst's own boss. Unfortunately, the staging of the meeting often leads to a performance or show. Understandably, the analyst wants to look knowledgeable in front of colleagues and wants to be professionally courteous to the CEO to ensure ongoing access to the company's senior executive team. Even when a tough, challenging question is courageously attempted, most CEOs have the politician's talent for delivering lengthy, evasive filibusters for answers. I have witnessed many hour-long meetings where there was time for only half a dozen questions due to the length of the answers.

One should take several steps to have a more productive meeting in which disconfirming evidence is sought. First, it is helpful if the primary interviewer puts together a list of questions or agenda topics and circulates it to colleagues who will be attending. This gives colleagues the opportunity to suggest additional topics or to reframe questions.

It is possible to go too far with the prep questions, though, which can lead to a rigid conversation lacking the opportunity to make live pivots to more interesting topics that arise. I recall a meeting with the CEO of eBay, which we were considering as a new investment at Goldman Sachs. Our technology analyst at the time was a particularly regimented fellow who had put a list of several dozen questions together that ran two pages and was divided into three sections. The meeting began, and he led off with the first question on the page, asked exactly as he had worded it. After receiving the answer and jotting down notes, he moved on to the second question and asked that one verbatim. Midway through the meeting, the CEO was answering a question, and his eyes lit up as he touched on a new business venture, expressing a lot of enthusiasm. My analyst cut him off, saying, "Can you hold that thought until later in the meeting? I have questions on that topic, but they are in my third section." We were on the verge of hearing about something important and interesting, and the analyst was so tied to his agenda that he requested we not be told about it!

I have also found it helpful to invite a fixed-income colleague to a meeting with management. Corporate management teams, like professional politicians, often have the skill of telling each audience what it wants to hear. When discussing priorities for free cash flow, the equity investor might hear about stock buybacks or growth-oriented capital spending plans. The debt investor will hear about the importance of a pristine balance sheet and the paydown of outstanding borrowings. By having the stock and bond investors in the room at the same time, a more neutral story is likely to be told and heard.

Over the years, both at Goldman Sachs and Eaton Vance, our teams received training from retired government intelligence agents and police interrogators. This included how to sequence and phrase questions and how to interpret body language. For example, the early questions in an interview might be easy and friendly to establish a rhythm, and then the prompt question would come, and it would be phrased in a nonstandard way. Rather than asking, "Is there anything wrong with Division X of your company?" the question might be phrased as, "Who have you put in charge of fixing the problems in Division X?" which assumes the conclusion and has the effect of creating a minor complexity that the respondents have to sort out on the fly. They have to either accept your assumption or challenge it, which will make for a more insightful answer.

How a respondent physically reacts to the prompt question can be revealing. There is typically a brief delay immediately after the prompt, possibly followed by a minor physiological reaction. When lying or responding to an uncomfortable question, humans often become physically uncomfortable and will shift their bodies in predictable ways. These movements could include crossing one's arms, covering one's mouth with the hand, leaning backward, or if seated, shifting to a new position in the chair. When using these techniques, it can be useful to have a colleague monitor the responses while the interviewer focuses on the questions.

As an investment team leader who was not the first point of contact with the management teams of our investment holdings, I told our analysts that I was always willing to play "bad cop" if they had an aggressive question that they wanted to have asked but wished to protect their own relationship with the company. I can recall our energy-sector analyst at Goldman Sachs taking me up on this during an interview with Christophe de Margerie, CEO of Total, the French oil major. She prepped me as follows: "When you hear me ask question [X], he is going to give me answer [Y]. I don't want to let him off the hook with that answer, but they will stop taking my calls if I ask the question I really want to ask, so when we reach that point in the conversation, I want you to interrupt with follow-up question [Z]." She knew the company and this CEO well, and that was exactly how the conversation unfolded.[4]

I have attended company management meetings at industry conferences where analysts from hedge funds were also in the room. Their questions were typically short term in nature and often annoyed the management team, who were more interested in discussing strategy and the multiyear outlook.

The other thing that I found irritating about hedge fund analysts is that they always seemed to bring a laptop or iPad with a keyboard to a shared meeting. While the member of the management team was answering a question, there was the hedge fund analyst, head down, banging hard on a keyboard like a chimpanzee doing a crude impersonation of a court reporter. One portfolio manager with whom I worked taught me an important lesson. She was interviewing the CEO of a midsized bank and asked a provocative question; the CEO paused and seemed uncertain of whether to answer. Calmly, she said, "I am putting my pen down," and she literally laid her writing utensil next to her pad of paper, indicating that he could speak freely without fear of there being a written transcription.[5]

Since we don't know what we don't know, I am a big fan of the open-ended question as a way of pursuing disconfirming information. A few of my favorites include: What have I not asked you that I should have? What are you most worried about over the next year? What were the top three topics that your board of directors were focused on at the last board meeting? If we meet again in five years and your vision has not come to fruition, what will be the most likely reason? If you were starting from scratch with a blank sheet of paper, how might your company look?

Eaton Vance's equity analysts regularly received compliments from CEOs and CFOs after a meeting with us. They would remark on the fact that we had portfolio managers in attendance on our side of the table, and the nature of the questions was longer-term in nature and more engaging.

Confirmation bias might be the most difficult bias to overcome. After all, it feels good to receive or interpret information that is consistent with our prior beliefs. On the other hand, it is unsettling to learn that we might be wrong, particularly about something that is important to us. For this reason, I believe that the best way to seek out disconfirming evidence is with the assistance of a partner or partners acting as devil's advocate. If the culture of the relationship or team is such that all the members understand that it is their responsibility to disagree with one another and to vet uncertain ideas, this assignment should come naturally.

One newly available tool for the individual who recognizes the need to seek out disconfirming information as part of the investment process, or seeks truly critical feedback on an idea, is the artificial intelligence (AI) chatbot in the form of ChatGPT, Claude, Grok, and others. One nice feature of these tools is that you can instruct them as to the tone and level of sophistication you want. For example, I recently fed ChatGPT my investment thesis on a stock that I like and instructed it to "give me your best arguments on why I am wrong." It came up with seven reasons, each with subbullets. While some of these were generic and likely reflected consensus thinking, this exercise helped me ensure that I was not blind to something obvious and known by others.

If working alone, try reprogramming your own mindset. During the summer that I spent as an MBA intern at Fidelity, one of the firm's most respected fund managers hosted an internal luncheon to offer his advice to the analysts in the department. His words stuck with me: "I believe it is the job of an equity analyst to diligently work to develop a thesis on a stock. Once they have that thesis, they should spend every waking moment trying to prove it wrong."

SOLUTION SUMMARY

1. **Ask open-ended questions.** The more narrowly tailored your question, the less likely you will receive an answer outside the scope of what you are expecting.
2. **Phrase questions neutrally.** Don't give away your preconceptions to the person or search engine. Or go further and disguise your inclination by adopting the opposite point of view.
3. **Use the 2-4-6 test.** When evaluating potential new hires, use tests that include the original one designed to identify those who are predisposed to search for disconfirming evidence.

Chapter Twelve

ANALYSIS PARALYSIS

Patience is power. Patience is not an absence of action.
—Fulton J. Sheen, American bishop

Not to decide is to decide.
—Harvey Cox, American theologian

JEFF BEZOS has advice for how a large company can fend off "Day 2" and continue to innovate and act like a start-up on "Day 1." He argues that an important element of maintaining a Day 1 culture is for the organization to make high-quality decisions quickly:

> First, never use a one-size-fits-all decision-making process. Many decisions are reversible, two-way doors. Those decisions can use a light-weight process. For those, so what if you're wrong? . . .
>
> Second, most decisions should probably be made with somewhere around 70 percent of the information you wish you had. If you wait for 90 percent, in most cases, you're probably being slow. Plus, either way, you need to be good at quickly recognizing and correcting bad decisions. If you're good at course correcting, being wrong may be less costly than you think . . .[1]

Bezos's second point—the idea that one should often make decisions with incomplete information—is difficult for many people to accept. In the setting of professional investing, most equity analysts are strong at math and working with spreadsheets. They take comfort in the precision of numbers. I have heard many analysts say some version of, "Let's wait for the earnings report so that I can update my model" or "I'll decide after hearing what management has to say at their Investor Day." This desire to accumulate more information sometimes risks missing a fleeting opportunity.

Analysis paralysis may not technically be a cognitive bias, but it still gets in the way of good decision making. The concept, if not the term, of *analysis paralysis* can be found throughout history in *Aesop's Fables* ("The Fox and the Cat"), Shakespeare (Hamlet's indecisiveness soliloquy "To be, or not to be"), and Voltaire ("The perfect is the enemy of the good").

Researchers have described how the presence of too many options for a consumer can be overwhelming and lead to lower satisfaction.[2] When I first heard of this concept, I resisted it. How could more choice be bad? It seemed un-American. I have since come to appreciate the value of simplicity when facing a decision of minor consequence. When standing in the spice aisle of the grocery store, how much do you really benefit from the plethora of choices: table salt, sea salt, pink Himalayan salt, kosher salt, and endless other varieties?

Researchers agree that when a person faces too much information or too many choices, anxiety may ensue. The result is less contentment and more difficulty in reaching a conclusion.

A cognitive bias that is related to analysis paralysis is the "ambiguity effect." This occurs when people prefer a known outcome to an equally valuable outcome with variance or uncertainty. This bias was identified by economist Daniel Ellsberg.[3] He described the thought experiment of a person predicting the color of a ball drawn from one of two urns for the prize of $100. In the first urn, you are told that there are an equal number of red and black balls, yielding a 50 percent probability of winning. In the second urn, you are told that there are red and black balls of an unknown proportion. Ellsberg reasoned that many people would prefer selecting a ball from the first urn since the proportionate mix is known with certainty. Since the second urn could have a mix ranging from 0/100 to 100/0, the expected probability of either color remains 50/50, making it an equally good option, but one that many individuals will avoid due to the "ambiguity." This preference for certainty over ambiguity leads many people to seek to accumulate ever more information and data long past the point of it providing any incremental value.

Over the course of my career, I noticed a preference for inaction whenever there was a broad market sell-off. I came to realize that these were the times for a less democratic approach to managing the portfolio, and I would assert myself with more direct authority and less deference to others. Because we favored high-quality companies, defined as those with high returns on capital and strong balance sheets, our portfolios typically had a modest defensive posture and would perform relatively well in a downturn. I say *relatively* well because most of our positions would still fall in value but be down less than the broad market. Since our stocks had fallen in price, the level of price potential upside to reach our price target's estimate of intrinsic value would improve, and our analysts would not be inclined to sell. It would feel like jumping out of the frying pan into the fire to part ways with something that we knew well and still liked to buy a lower-quality company that had plummeted in price. The risk to the portfolio was that if/when things bottomed out, the subsequent rally would likely be led by a different group of stocks than those that had held up relatively well. In these situations, I would adopt my former boss's words: "The deck has been reshuffled." This meant that the opportunity set today is different from the one that was available when we first made our decisions to buy our current holdings. It is important not to take too much comfort in what we own if better opportunities are revealing themselves.

I also found that one way of dealing with analysis paralysis is simply to split the difference. I would say to a member of our team, "We know enough to get started with a position in this stock for the portfolio. Let's buy half of our target weight now and fill out the rest of it after you have learned more. If your further analysis turns up a risk or concern, we will simply sell out and look for a different opportunity." These "starter positions" turned the ambiguity and endowment effects on their heads, flipping these biases from vices into virtues. I have found that once a stock is owned in the portfolio—as opposed to being on a watch list or in a paper/model portfolio—it becomes real, and the analyst accelerates the work to get completely on top of it.

There are three variables that must be in place for the starter-position approach to work well. First, transactional or frictional costs must be low. For example, it would not be a good idea to say, "Let's go ahead and build half of that factory that we have been discussing. We'll figure out whether it is worth completing later." When buying and selling large-cap US stocks, transaction costs are typically low. The best transaction cost analysis models that I have seen suggest that for an asset management firm with a professional trading desk, the all-in cost to trade (i.e., commissions, bid/ask spreads, exchange fees, market impact from the footprint of our own trade) is about 0.25 percent (i.e., 25 basis points) of the total dollar amount being traded. Even at this size, transaction costs can accumulate over the course of the year, so they are not to be ignored, but they are sufficiently small in percentage terms to allow the occasional reversal of an initial decision. Frictional costs can also take the form of sacrificing the value of alternative options. Using an example from everyday life, opting to buy that expensive new coat today forgoes the opportunity to buy an even-more desirable one later if it goes on sale, so it should be conceded that making speedy decisions is not completely cost free.

The second requirement is that it must be understood at the beginning that there is a possibility that the decision will be reversed, and there should be no shame in that outcome. In the investment business, where conviction and confidence are cherished, this can be difficult, and the leader must be clear about what is going on. For example, the investor might say to colleagues, "Due to this morning's sharp selloff in stock [XYZ], we will be starting a position. However, if our due diligence over the next week turns up red flags, we will be happy to exit, whether we have a gain or loss, and free up cash for other uses."

Third, it should be made clear that the starter position is a half-measure, not a final resting place. For risk-averse members of the team, it might otherwise be easy to let a series of partial decisions accumulate. I was willing to buy a starter position of up to 1 percent (i.e., 100 basis points) of the total portfolio value, followed soon thereafter by a formal presentation of the stock, where we were predisposed to own more.

Small, half-sized positions in the portfolio can accumulate not only from unfinished starter positions, but from winners that have been trimmed, holdings that have been cut due to the accumulation of risk concerns, or those that have been reduced to free up cash for other opportunities. It becomes necessary on occasion to deal with this tail of small positions.[4] One of our investment leaders developed the portfolio exercise, "One up, one out." Each member of the team was required to identify a current portfolio holding that they would support making a larger weight, and one that they would like to see eliminated entirely. This exercise forced a discussion of the smaller positions and led to a positive bias to action.

I experienced the benefits of the starter-position approach for myself as a gas utility analyst at Fidelity in 2000. Midway through my summer internship, I found myself giving a two-minute oral pitch to one of the fund managers on the common stock of Equitable Resources (stock symbol EQT), a Pennsylvania firm that owned natural gas exploration and production assets as well as a gas utility. While I was still standing in the doorway of his office, he turned around, picked up the phone, hit a speed-dial button for the in-house Fidelity equity trading desk, and said, "Buy me 100,000 shares of EQT."

My first thought was to be struck by his quick decision, and my ego was boosted by this show of confidence in my recommendation. My next thought was to feel a sudden increase in responsibility for this new position and what it would mean for the shareholders in his fund. It was now real.

In addition to timelier decisions, another benefit of the starter position or split-the-difference approach is that it takes some of the pressure off. I worked with one portfolio manager who ran concentrated portfolios and did not want to bring a new position into the portfolio until it was worthy of a 3 percent (i.e., 300 basis points) weight. This led members of the team to keep their new ideas closely guarded, lest they wake up one day to find that a large position had been bought before they were ready to back it fully.

The desire to complete 100 percent of the analysis before acting can be the result of risk aversion and analysis paralysis, but it can also stem from simply wanting to look informed in front of colleagues. Fears of being perceived as sloppy or lacking expertise can lead people to delay decisions that they know they will have to explain or defend. The desire to have a polished presentation, with all the loose ends tied up and good answers to every potential question, can act like sand in the gears of a timely decision-making process. Reluctance to share one's work-in-progress has the deleterious effect of denying valuable insights to colleagues or keeping the manager at bay early in the idea development phase. I have seen analysts withhold information when they know they want to sell a position but have not yet completed the work on its replacement; from the portfolio manager's perspective, the replacement opportunity could be ready to go but be from another sector.

Tools that I have used to encourage junior colleagues to show their work include holding a meeting where "half-baked ideas" are discussed. The pressure comes off, as everyone is required to bring at least one unpolished idea. The next steps include putting these half-baked ideas on a "working list" and then following up on each one on a specific date, two weeks hence.

Practicing making decisions in low-stakes situations is another good way to build the muscle of decisiveness. I have recommended to new analysts the idea of keeping a decision journal or diary. After every piece of work done on a stock, write down "Buy" or "Sell," along with the price. You just listened to an earnings call? Buy or sell? You just finished updating your Microsoft Excel spreadsheet model? Buy or sell? You attended the company's investor day? Buy or sell? By making small decisions and reviewing the outcomes, you can train yourself to take a stand.[5]

A more formal variation of the decision journal in asset management is the analyst paper portfolio. The analyst manages a phantom portfolio of stocks and has full discretion of what to buy or sell and how much. At Eaton Vance, we called these "Analyst Select Portfolios (ASPs)." We would track the performance of these ASPs precisely by using the formal attribution system that we used for client reporting in real-money accounts. I was a strong advocate for the ASP and included it in the analyst's scorecard at the end of the year for judging performance and making bonus decisions. As I saw it, the ASP served several purposes:

- It represented training and practice for analysts who wanted more autonomy or the opportunity to become a portfolio manager down the line.

- It was an independent assessment of the analyst's performance without the fingerprints and biases of the portfolio managers.
- It allowed the analyst to express a level of precise conviction in a way that the words, "I reiterate my buy recommendation" do not.
- It offered a view into how well the portfolio managers were performing, given the raw material with which they had to work.

Several colleagues expressed reservations about the ASPs, arguing that analysts could game the result by trading their ASPs late in the day or buying stocks that were outside the client remit or guidelines, but I believe that the benefits outweighed these potential shortcomings.

While not analysis paralysis per se, another potential source of decision delay is when a cultural standard of overly formal, lengthy, written material becomes the norm for internal discussions. It is one thing to insist on professional-quality materials for interactions with clients, it is quite another to do the same for in-house meetings. A pet peeve of mine is when I see the company logo at the top of a slide and the footnote, "internal use only" at the bottom. I think, "Why did this person take the time to put the logo on this document? Do they think that I do not know the name of the company for which we both work?"

Overly formal, internal presentation materials are most common when the presenter is below the recipient in the firm's hierarchy. Understandably, the junior accountant's budget presentation to the CEO may be their once-a-year opportunity to be in front of the big boss. In this case, it is the CEO's responsibility to say, "Please spend your time on ensuring the figures are accurate rather than putting polish on a fancy presentation or inundating me with unnecessary information. Let's focus on the key numbers and have a fulsome discussion."

Peter Lynch, who managed Fidelity's Magellan Fund in the 1980s, was fond of saying that one ought to be able to clearly articulate the merits of a potential investment in just two minutes. This required analysts to have a depth of understanding of the business being evaluated such that they could quickly get to the key points. It takes a level of self-confidence and willingness to be vulnerable to avoid the temptation to hide behind extraneous data or show off how much inconsequential information one knows.

An investment banker colleague at Goldman Sachs told me that on one business pitch, he had been instructed by the prospective client not to come with more than a dozen slides in the deck of materials. "We will rip out anything after page 12 and toss it in the trash bin." Under this constraint, the banker and his colleagues were forced to winnow the message down to its essence. After the meeting, all involved agreed that it was the best pitch deck they had ever constructed.[6]

At asset management firms, internal discussions of potential investment ideas are often conducted with the aid of supporting written materials. When I first arrived at Eaton Vance, the investment presentations often took the form of Microsoft PowerPoint and ran for thirty or more slides. I quickly put a ten-page limit in place and discouraged the use of PowerPoint and its formality.

In my opinion, it is also important to have materials for internal discussion distributed ahead of time. We used a two-day rule. If the materials were not ready two days prior to the scheduled discussion, then it would be postponed to a later date. We asked each member of the team to read the materials ahead of time and to submit questions in writing. This ensured that everyone was prepared and ready to engage in a deeper level of discussion and debate.

Jeff Bezos reached a similar conclusion for meetings at Amazon and Blue Origin:

> I like a crisp document and a messy meeting . . . A typical meeting will start with a six-page narratively structured memo. And we do study hall. For 30 minutes, we sit there silently together in the meeting and read . . . And then we discuss . . . We are all on the same page. We've all read the memo . . . Now we can have a really elevated discussion.
>
> This is so much better than a slide show presentation . . . One of the problems is PowerPoint is really designed to persuade. It's kind of a sales tool. Internally, the last thing you want to do is sell. You are truth seeking. You are trying to find truth.[7]

Finally, when faced with a decision, consider whether extra data is likely to make a difference to the ultimate course of action. I recall a professor in one of my undergraduate Economics classes illustrating this concept with the following example:

> Suppose you have a final exam coming up. You have decided that if you do well on the test, you will reward yourself with a trip to Hawaii. However, if you perform poorly, you will be inclined to nurse your disappointment with a trip . . . to Hawaii. You decide to hold off on booking your flight until you get the test result back. In the meantime, the price of the airline ticket goes up.

This example illustrates the ambiguity effect mentioned earlier. The extra information does not change the decision, but it gives psychological comfort that more information is known.

I witnessed the impact of the ambiguity effect on markets in the summer of 2004. It was July, and stock prices had been languishing, down modestly from the start of the year. I got up from my office chair and walked over to our equity trading desk to chat with our traders:

> Me: "What are you guys seeing and hearing?"
>
> Trader: "No one wants to take risk right now. We have the Olympics coming up in Athens in a couple of weeks. There are concerns of a potential terrorist attack. In November, we have the presidential election and the possibility that we will have a repeat of 2000, where the winner was not known for several weeks."

Hearing this made me more positive toward stocks. I thought, "If those are the reasons that stocks have been a bit weak, I should be buying now. After all, in a couple of weeks, we will know whether a terrorist event has happened at the Olympics, and in only four months, Election Day will have occurred, and I am willing to bet we will know the winner one way or the other." In effect, I was using the time traveler mental framing to imagine whether these risks and anxieties would still be with us in a few weeks and months.

This chapter would not be complete without acknowledging the drawbacks of the opposite of analysis paralysis, sometimes called "extinction by instinct." In other words, quick decisions are not always best.

It is important to identify those decisions that are nonstraightforward and irreversible. These require a deeper level of analysis. With these decisions, you should slow down. Force yourself to defer the decision until it has been properly vetted. Sleep on it.

Finally, I concede that there are times when the virtue of patience should be preferred to immediate action. Perhaps new opportunities will emerge that will not be available if one has already made a commitment. Maybe a truly important piece of information will soon be learned, and the current option will still be available, so there is little to no cost to wait. In other cases, the status quo is preferable to any alternative.[8] The grass is not always greener. This concept of action bias is explored in chapter 13.

SOLUTION SUMMARY

1. **Split the difference with small positions.** Use the concept of a small starter position to put things in motion and make inertia your friend while continuing the analytical process.
2. **Practice making low-stakes decisions.** Utilize exercises like "one up, one out" to force a decision. Document actions that would have been taken if you had the authority. Build a paper model and record results over time.
3. **Simplify.** Eliminate unlikely choices and extraneous information. Avoid PowerPoint for internal discussions.

Chapter Thirteen

ACTION BIAS

Action is the foundational key to all success.
—Pablo Picasso

Don't just do something, stand there.
—The White Rabbit, *Alice in Wonderland*

ON JULY 9, 2006, in Berlin, the French national soccer team faced their Italian counterparts in the FIFA World Cup final, the last match of French superstar Zinedine Zidane's illustrious soccer career. The match is famous for the red card given to Zidane in the 110th minute following his head butt of Italian defender Marco Materazzi, who had insulted Zidane's sister. Extra time ended with the match tied at 1–1, so it went to a shootout, which Italy won 5–3 on kicks from the penalty spot.

Largely forgotten in the history of the match is the successful penalty kick taken by Zidane in the seventh minute. As Zidane planted his left foot next to the ball, Italian goalkeeper Gianluigi Buffon began diving to his right. Zidane's right foot struck the ball softly, and it floated up the middle, hit the underside of the crossbar, and bounced on the opposite side of the goal line as Buffon watched helplessly from the ground. The British announcers described the kick as "audacious" and "mighty cheeky." This form of penalty kick is known as a "Panenka," named after Antonin Panenka, who used it to win the European Championship for Czechoslovakia in 1976.

The sports analytics community has studied penalty kicks extensively. Although soccer is generally a fluid game, the penalty kick is unique in that it involves only one player from each of the two teams in a strictly controlled situation, like a pitcher and hitter in baseball. The optimal strategy for the kicker and keeper is a function of what the other person is likely to do, so film of prior penalty kicks is often studied, game theory is used, and a so-called mixed strategy is employed by each player to avoid becoming predictable to the opponent. However, goalkeepers almost always choose to dive preemptively. In fact, it has been argued that standing still is the goalkeeper's optimal strategy.[1] So, why don't they do that? Action bias.

In the face of stress or risk, it is human nature to act. Doing nothing feels wrong. However, having a bias to action does not always result in a better outcome. In the case of professional soccer goalkeepers, they are highly incentivized and encounter the penalty kick situation on a regular basis, so it is in their interest to spend time developing an optimal strategy, which would include mixing in periodically staying in the middle of the goal. InnerDrive, a British science education blog, cites two studies on penalty kicks.[2] In one, analysis of 999 penalties in the German Bundesliga found that 15 percent of the time, the kicker shoots down the middle. The second study of 286 penalty kicks in top leagues from around the world found that goalkeepers remain in the center only 2 percent of the time.

An early mention of the term *action bias* comes from Anthony Patt and Richard Zeckhauser, who used surveys of hypothetical questions to study action bias in environmental decisions by policymakers.[3] They concluded that the incentives and rewards for the decision maker are to take some form of action regardless of whether the likely outcome of the decision is positive. In other words, politicians personally benefit from being seen to be doing something . . . anything.

One area where action bias in political leaders can be observed is in the rankings of past US presidents by historians. For those who favor a hands-off, limited federal government, Calvin Coolidge ranks high on their lists. Nicknamed "Silent Cal," he was president during the 1920s.[4] During his administration, he cut taxes and balanced the budget, and the economy grew at 7 percent per year, but in other respects, he was quiet and inactive. Despite his successes, he is labeled a "do-nothing" president by many and was ranked twenty-fourth out of forty-four presidents in a recent survey of 142 historians and other scholars of the US presidency.[5]

There are various theories on the source of action bias. Asymmetrical rewards and incentives for action over inaction constitute one theory. Another idea is that there are evolutionary causes.[6] The "fight or flight" response speaks to this bias for action.

The word "churn" has a negative connotation when applied to Wall Street. Old-style, commission-based stockbrokers were sometimes accused of churning their clients' accounts to generate commissions. They were paid when a transaction occurred (i.e., a stock, bond, or mutual fund was bought or sold), which created an incentive to generate activity regardless of whether it was in their clients' best interest. The industry has evolved, and stockbrokers now call themselves "financial advisors." Although commissions still exist, the more popular model, known as "advisory," is to charge the client a small percentage of the assets under management (usually less than 1 percent per year) regardless of any activity occurring within the account. Arguably, this fee arrangement reduces much of the incentive for action.

Of the various biases discussed in this book, action bias is the one that I believe I personally suffer from the most. I have even worn it proudly at times, encouraging colleagues to get to a firm decision with phrases like, "Let's have a bias to act." I often behaved as though I believed that patience is a vice not a virtue, with impetuousness as the outcome. Perhaps this is because I have seen it as my job to combat analysis paralysis or to provide impetus to inertia.

Chapter 1, on the endowment effect, discussed the benefit of harvesting tax losses as an antidote to loss aversion. While the US federal tax code provides an incentive to cut losers, it also provides an incentive for inaction with winners. Investments held for twelve months have a lower tax rate applied to any realized gain, while waiting even longer defers the tax hit indefinitely. In fact, if a person holds an appreciated asset all the way until death, the beneficiaries of the estate receive a step-up in cost basis and will never pay capital gains taxes on those unrealized gains.

I believe that I learned to be more patient upon taking over responsibility for tax-managed mutual funds at Eaton Vance. In one specific case, I took over the direct management of a tax-sensitive mutual fund that had a position in United Healthcare that had appreciated more than tenfold. During my eight years managing the fund, I never traded that position, and it continued to outperform the broad stock market. This was a form of forced inaction.

One of the attributes of a career in asset management that appealed to me was the precision of performance measurement. The only job that I can think of with a similar level of precise daily feedback on how you are performing is that of a hitter in Major League Baseball (MLB). In the case of stock picking, one's investment performance, the equivalent of a batting average, is publicly available for the world to see each day. There is no hiding from it. There may be plenty of reasons, explanations, and excuses, but the number is the number. In most other jobs, the measure of an individual's performance comes down to the subjective assessment of the boss.

The daily measurement of performance is turned into quarterly and annual attribution scorecards for the purpose of reporting results to clients. Quantitative approaches like Brinson attribution and Barra risk models attribute the sources of performance and exposures to factors such as sector classification, momentum, leverage, market beta, market capitalization, and stock-specific elements. I have found that one of the attributes of the most successful investors is their eagerness to study the results of their decisions as reflected in these attribution reports.

Shortly after joining Eaton Vance, I took over responsibility for the management of the firm's large-cap value strategies. Existing clients were understandably sensitive to any changes that I might be inclined to make. One change that they observed was that portfolio turnover rose. On an annualized basis, it had been running just below 50 percent (implying an average holding period of two years), but with my hand on the tiller, turnover rose to about 80 percent. I wanted to be able to explain to clients and myself that all this activity was adding value. I asked one of our performance attribution analysts to run a report showing how the portfolio that I inherited would have performed had I left it static. After about one year, we compared the actual portfolio to the hypothetical buy-and-hold portfolio. Both had performed well, but the live portfolio had done more than 100 basis points (i.e., 1 percent) better. We continued to run versions of this analysis and came to refer to it as the "Where the Rubber Meets the Road" report. Occasionally, there were short periods of time where our cumulative actions had resulted in a portfolio that actually trailed the buy-and-hold version. It is quite humbling to be told that if you had simply gone to the beach or sat on the couch, your clients would have been financially better off.

These different methods of analyzing one's own track record and the decisions that go into it are all forms of postmortems. Good or bad, regular debriefing is the cornerstone of a strong decision-making process.

Finally, it is important to draw a distinction between decision delay and intentional inaction. With decision delay, you still plan to take action in the future, but you believe that the decision will benefit from collecting more information or waiting for new opportunities to open up (such as a better price on a stock). With intentional inaction, however, the decision has been made, and that decision is not to act.

SOLUTION SUMMARY

1. **Keep a decision journal.** Think of inaction as a form of decision. Write down that you have assertively decided to take no action and own the outcome.
2. **Debrief the mission.** Study the track record of your decisions. Would you have performed the same, or even better, if you had been less active?
3. **Take advantage of natural circuit breakers.** In an investment setting, such circuit breakers might be tax code incentives for inaction. In other scenarios, they could include a process that requires written documentation or approvals that slow things down before action is taken.

Chapter Fourteen

OPTIMISM BIAS

The glass is half full.

—Josiah Stamp, British statistician and banker, 1935

The glass is half empty.

—Josiah Stamp, British statistician and banker, 1935

IN THE 1970S, Boston's urban planners became concerned with downtown traffic congestion. Specifically, I-93 cut through the heart of Boston as an elevated highway, which exacerbated traffic problems. A second interstate, I-90, known locally as the "Mass Pike," had no direct route to Logan Airport. In 1982, planning began for a megaproject to relieve these and other problems. In April 1987, with the vocal support of the speaker of the US House of Representatives—and Boston/Cambridge native—Tip O'Neill, Congress passed the Surface Transportation and Uniform Relocation Assistance Act of 1987. Among other things, this provided funding for Boston's Central Artery/Tunnel Project, which came to be known colloquially as "The Big Dig."

The Big Dig had an initial cost estimate of $2.8 billion and was scheduled to be completed in 1998. The project broke ground in 1991. After an initial burst of enthusiasm, reality began to set in. The Big Dig infamously became the most expensive highway project in the history of the United States. It experienced countless problems, delays, and cost overruns. When the project was finally completed in December 2007, about a decade late, the bill was $8.08 billion, nearly three times the original estimate. In their eagerness to get the project greenlit, the city planners had been far too optimistic about the timeline and ultimate cost.

In 1991, the same year as construction began on the Big Dig, three friends and I made our first pilgrimage to Las Vegas to deploy our newly acquired blackjack card-counting skills. (We were nineteen and twenty years old, but the casinos did not check IDs back then.) Late on the second night, one friend came up to the rest of us to announce that he had discovered a one-dollar minimum, single-deck blackjack game across the street at the Oasis, which was attached to the Dunes casino.[1] As we walked down the Strip, my friend said, "I cannot believe I have denied myself this Mecca of Money for so long!" We still have fun occasionally saying this phrase to one another all these years later.

On the six-hour drive back to Santa Barbara that Sunday afternoon, our group of four college students engaged in a meandering conversation about many things. At one point, one friend asked the obnoxious question, "Which one of us do you think will be most successful in our careers?" We each picked ourselves. Optimism and self-confidence ran high.

Optimism bias is the tendency to believe that uncertain future events will have positive outcomes. A certain amount of optimism is healthy, but too much of it can lead to disappointment. We often view optimistic people in a more positive light than pessimists. No one wants to spend time with "Debbie Downer." Like several of the other cognitive biases that we have discussed so far, a little bit is OK, but too much can lead to problems.

The concept of optimism has been around for a long time, but excessive optimism is a more recent discovery. In 1980, psychologist Neil Weinstein coined the term "unrealistic optimism."[2] He conducted a study of 200 college students in which each student was asked to rank whether their own chances of experiencing a particular life event differed from those of their classmates. Examples of positive life events from the study included "lik[ing] your postgraduation job," "living past 80," and "having a mentally gifted child." Examples of negative life events included "having a drinking problem," "dropping out of college," and "car turns out to be a lemon," among others. There were forty-two life events in total.

In the study, the subjects tended to put a high relative probability on positive events coming to pass, while they underweighted the likelihood of negative events occurring to themselves relative to their classmates. The positive event with the most extreme skew was "owning your own home," where there were six times as many optimistic versus pessimistic answers. On the negative side of the ledger, the most extreme level of optimism was in rating the odds of being "divorced a few years after married," which had a 9.5-to-1 ratio.

Reasons for the excessive optimism included perceived controllability and giving insufficient weight to the motivations and maneuvers of others. In a second study, 120 female students from the first study were asked to write down the factors that would influence their chances for eight future events. This information was given to a second group of students. The level of optimism in this second group fell significantly once they became aware of their classmates' supporting arguments.

A joke about marriage goes as follows: "50 percent of all marriages end in divorce; the other half end in death." As Weinstein found in his study, young lovers can be overly optimistic about their odds of marital longevity. At the risk of being overly analytical or cynical about such a question, individuals considering marriage who wish to evaluate their odds of success would do well to use the base rate for all marriages as a starting point rather than starting from the perspective of their own relationship studied in a vacuum.

Base rates can be used for any question where there is reliable historical data to use as a guide. What are the odds of a small business finding success? What are the chances that you will like your first job? How likely is it that your child, who is a star athlete, will go on to play their sport professionally? These are all questions that can easily be answered for the population at large. Even if you have reason to believe that your personal situation differs from the general rule, having a baseline can help temper excessive optimism.

In investing, optimism tends to be at its highest in economic sectors like information technology and biotechnology. A new innovation or cure for a disease drives an exciting narrative that gets the blood flowing. A good way for investors to manage their optimism is through the time-tested tool of diversification. As the saying goes, rather than putting all of one's eggs in a single basket, spread the risk (and the opportunity) across multiple investments. For a small-cap growth portfolio manager, this means being willing to own a basket of, say, eight to twelve small positions in an exciting but highly risky subindustry.

Having the humility to admit that you cannot predict the future with precision will lead to success with this approach if just one of these positions turns out to be a ten-bagger; this will be true even if half of the remainder go bankrupt.

Military leaders and cybersecurity professionals guard against complacency and overconfidence by conducting red-team/blue-team drills. One team is assigned the role of attacking the other. They look for weak points and overlooked vulnerabilities.

Try writing a "premortem." This is an idea that I first heard from Michael Mauboussin.[3] Imagine that the decision has already been made and things have gone horribly wrong. Why did this happen? Risks and disconfirming data that might have otherwise been brushed to the side will suddenly be in the spotlight and can be given full consideration.

SOLUTION SUMMARY

1. **Beware the base rate.** This is sometimes called the "outside view." Study similar projects and decisions to understand the success rate of a broad sample set.
2. **Conduct red-team/blue-team drills.** This is a form of devil's advocacy, but it is more formal and project- or scenario-based. Ask the adversary to try to undermine your idea and identify weaknesses.
3. **Prebrief with premortems.** Assume failure and work backward. What went wrong? This is best done with the help of friends or colleagues who may not share your optimism.

Chapter Fifteen

OVERCONFIDENCE

Le courage de son opinion.

—1800s French phrase that translates in modern English as "courage of one's convictions."

What gets us into trouble is not what we don't know. It's what we know for sure that just ain't so.

—Mark Twain, nineteenth- century author

"THERE'S NO EXCUSE. I've got to be smarter." These were the words of Arizona Cardinals running back Emari Demercado after he scampered seventy-two yards in an apparent touchdown against the Tennessee Titans in week 5 of the 2025 National Football League (NFL) season. However, after video replay review, the touchdown was taken off the scoreboard, as it was revealed that Demercado had begun his celebration early by releasing the ball prior to crossing the goal line. The Cardinals went on to lose the game. An amazing side note is that Adonai Mitchell of the Indianapolis Colts had committed a nearly identical mistake just a week earlier. Mitchell's teammate, Jonathan Taylor, had done the same thing the prior season. The Hulu show *Chad Powers* uses the premise of an early celebration fumble as the catalyst for the antihero's journey. At the moment of beginning their respective celebrations, these players were 100 percent confident that they would score. In each of these cases, the early celebrator's team lost the game.

We have all had the experience of being highly confident in ourselves or our expectation of how an event will unfold, only to be shocked by what came next. Pride goes before the fall.

In the popular vernacular, confidence is good and overconfidence bad. Confidence can lead one to act rather than demur. It also *feels* better to be confident than unsure. However, overconfidence can lead one to take unnecessary risks or make poor decisions. Like confidence, overconfidence also feels good unless future events unfold to reveal the hubris.

Overconfidence likely has certain societal benefits or positive externalities. Small businesses fail at a high rate. Entrepreneurial risk-taking, sometimes spurred by misplaced confidence in oneself or one's ideas, leads to the occasional breakthrough or innovation. Similarly, underconfidence, or self-doubt, is no virtue either. It can lead to excessive risk aversion, anxiety, and decision paralysis.

Overconfidence implies a level of confidence greater than that which is warranted. The warranted amount of confidence is a function of the uncertainty that exists. The higher the uncertainty, the lower one's confidence should be. The uncertainty could be that of one's knowledge of a factual matter from the past, or it could be the opinion that we have of our own prowess in certain endeavors. For example, in one study, a significant majority of people rated themselves as above-average drivers in terms of both skill and safety, which is a mathematical impossibility in the aggregate.[1] More often, overconfidence occurs with respect to the potential outcome of a future event. The future is inherently uncertain. For most people, particularly those prone to feelings of anxiety, this uncertainty is unwelcome. We don't like not knowing something. But overconfidence is particularly nefarious because it can work in tandem with any other bias by reinforcing it.

One way in which overconfidence can be empirically tested is to ask subjects to answer questions or make forecasts and then assign probabilities to their own answers. This test measures how well calibrated individuals are to their own forecasting accuracy levels. Researchers have found that most people overestimate their own accuracy.

Phil Tetlock, an academic with expertise on the topics of forecasting and decision making, has argued that there is a small percentage of the population that are "superforecasters," whose predictions are often better than experts with access to better information.[2] He and his colleagues developed a contest called the Good Judgment Project, where individuals could assess their own ability to forecast a variety of events. Individuals make predictions of the outcome of future events and assign probabilities to their forecasts. This is a great way to assess one's own forecasting ability and to calibrate one's confidence level to one's abilities.

A standard process in investment analysis is to develop a price target on a security. To move away from the false precision of pinpoint forecasts, my teams used probability-weighted price targets to determine potential prices one year hence. Typically, this involved developing three scenarios (although we also experimented with four and five). The three scenarios were the "bull case," "base case," and "bear case" for a stock. In real life, there are many more scenarios than this, but this was a manageable way of developing a sense of the range of plausible outcomes. For someone simply going through the motions on this exercise, this scenario analysis involved nothing more than varying a price-to-earnings (P/E) multiple that was being used to determine the price target. My preferred method was to start by contemplating a range of scenarios and writing a single sentence to describe that scenario. It might look like this for a bank stock:

- Bull case: The hiring of new commercial loan officers proves effective as loan growth picks up, which along with a steepening yield curve allows margins to expand and the balance sheet to grow, which drives higher earnings than currently expected and interest from potential mergers and acquisitions (M&A) suitors.
- Base case: Current trends persist, leading to mid-single-digit earnings per share (EPS) growth, along with a stable dividend. Credit risk remains benign.
- Bear case: Credit losses pick up, causing the bank to pull back on new loans, which leads to a 20 percent decline in EPS amid concerns about dividend coverage and capital levels.

After describing the scenarios qualitatively, one can select the appropriate valuation metric to use for each. In the example here, this might be an M&A takeout premium for the bull case, a P/E-based valuation for the base case, and a price-to–tangible book method for the bear case (since banks tend to be valued on this metric when in distress). In other words, the best way of thinking about the valuation that a stock might achieve in each situation is to understand how the stock would be valued under that scenario.

Finally, after developing three price targets, the analysts estimate the probability of each coming to pass. Then they compute the probability-weighted average of the three numbers to develop a final, blended price target.

I went through the effort of describing the process of developing probability-weighted price targets both to give you a peek into how professional investors approach valuation and scenario building, but also to show how this exercise can highlight overconfidence. For example, I recall on at least two occasions looking at an equity analyst's price targets to find a bear-case (i.e., realistic worst case) target that was 10 percent higher than the current stock price. In one case, the stock in question was that of a natural gas company whose fortunes were highly sensitive to energy prices; there was simply no way that a downside scenario of a steep fall in the company's share price could be off the table.

I cannot emphasize enough the importance of writing one's forecasts. The investment thesis, earnings model, and price targets are all forms of this documentation. If reviewed regularly, they are great tools for learning and making course corrections. It can help limit overconfidence if one reviews price targets from a year prior and sees that they forecast the bear case to be a price only 10 percent lower, but the stock has fallen 30 percent in the meantime. Likewise, if an analyst is overly cautious, a too-narrow range of outcomes will be revealed if the bull case proves too conservative. Calibration to reality is the goal.

A few years ago, I invited Dave Berke of Echelon Front, a leadership and development consulting firm, to speak with the Eaton Vance Equity Group on the topic of leadership and decision making under conditions of uncertainty. Berke is a retired US Marine Corps officer, fighter pilot, and ground combat leader, so he knows a lot about those topics. My two main takeaways from that discussion were "The debrief of a mission is the most important part" and "Leaders must set the example by being open about their mistakes."

We had already been using a portfolio exercise called "Public Confession: Two Mistakes I Made Last Year," which we did together as a team in our first meeting of the new year. After hearing Berke speak, I made a point of always going first. This exercise is also helpful in tempering overconfidence.

In an anthropology course that I took as an undergraduate at the University of California, Santa Barbara, we were studying the culture of an African tribe. Periodically, a small group of men would go on a hunt for the next meal. Once a kill had been made, the whole tribe would trek out to the carcass to retrieve the meat. They had a cultural practice of criticizing the hunter who had made the kill by saying things like, "This is a small animal that will not provide enough food for our village." The larger and more impressive the kill, the greater the negative feedback that would be given. When I first heard of this, my thought was, "That's just a bunch of collectivist nonsense. Negative incentives like that would not be effective in a Western society." However, I have come to appreciate the benefits of finding ways to keep the superstar's ego in check, lest they lose the edge that led to the success in the first place. The public confession of two mistakes is a way of accomplishing this.

Publicly admitting to mistakes as a method of checking hubris is helpful, but how can you calibrate your self-confidence to an accurate level? After all, the goal should not be to reduce confidence to the lowest level possible, but to match it to the underlying reality. One way to do this is to practice forecasting and making decisions by recording them along the way and reviewing them on a regular basis. This could be done in the form of a daily or weekly journal.

For an investment analyst, projections are a routine part of the job and are often made with precision. For example, an analyst might record in a journal, "I forecast that company [XYZ] will earn $1.30 cents per share next year, and I am 80 percent confident that the actual number will be within 15 cents per share of my forecast." In another example, a marketing executive who is confident of a new product launch might write, "I am 60 percent confident that sales in the first six months will exceed internal forecasts by at least 10 percent." Or the general manager (GM) of a professional sports team might write that the team's first-round draft pick will start in at least half the team's games next season, with a 75 percent level of confidence.

You can see that the application of this exercise is virtually limitless. Whether it is a business forecast, a sports prediction, or any other endeavor with a measure of uncertainty, this can be useful. The key points are that the prediction must be quantifiable and have a measurement date. There can be no room for subjective assessment after the fact.

To improve one's forecasting skill, it is important to understand the baseline probability of what is under consideration. For example, suppose that you are thinking about opening a new restaurant. You are highly motivated and confident that the location and cuisine that you have in mind will meet a market need. However, before proceeding, you decide to check the overall success rate of new restaurants in the United States. According to the National Restaurant Association, 60 percent of new restaurants fail in their first year, and 80 percent fail by year 5. In other words, there is a one-in-five chance of success over a five-year period. This baseline would not necessarily dissuade you from undertaking the venture, but it should dampen any excessive confidence and ensure that you understand all the points of potential failure.

Consider another example of using baseline data from the NFL. Suppose that you are the owner or GM of an NFL team. One of the other teams decided not to re-sign a star running back. The player is a well-known talent coming off a good season, who just turned twenty-eight years old. The rule of thumb is that running backs "hit a wall at age thirty," so you figure that this guy has at least two good performance years left before his production deteriorates. However, when you study the baseline closely, you see that in general, performance begins to deteriorate after a player turns age twenty-eight and drops significantly upon turning age thirty-one. Slightly more significant than age is historical workload, with production falling off meaningfully once a running back has had 1,750 career carries.[3] With this baseline information, you can make a more informed decision rather than overconfidently "trusting your own eyes" or "relying on your gut" to make it.

Throughout this book, we have discussed the value of having a devil's advocate. As mentioned earlier, a form of devil's advocate that has recently become available is artificial intelligence (AI), specifically large language models (LLMs) such as ChatGPT, Claude, Gemini, and Grok. With respect to an investment opportunity, for example, one can upload an investment thesis and other arguments in favor of a particular investment and instruct the AI tool to gather all publicly available information and make its best argument against the idea. One advantage of AI over humans in this capacity is that, if prompted properly, it will not be tempted to pull punches or be overly diplomatic in its critique.

SOLUTION SUMMARY

1. **Practice predictions.** Make forecasts explicit and measurable. Assign a probability. Review old forecasts and examine the level of accuracy. Adjust and fine-tune as you go.
2. **Make a public confession.** Identify mistakes that you made over the course of a project or period and share them with colleagues. Do this especially after success. If you are the leader, encourage others to do the same. A regular dose of humility tempers optimism.
3. **Prompt AI to be your biggest critic.** When feeling confident, ask an AI chatbot to give you its best arguments against your most cherished ideas.

INTERLUDE

From Bias to Collaboration

IN THE FIRST half of this book, we discussed fifteen biases—those arising from emotions, mental shortcuts, and human instincts—that work to undermine rational decisions. Most of these biases arise within the individual. But few decisions are made in isolation. Many are made around the table, as part of a team or committee.

Over the remaining chapters, we will focus on team dynamics. The impact of the group setting can be either helpful or harmful. It can provide important checks on our worst instincts or reinforce bias through collective blind spots and the pressure to conform.

We will explore the culture, structure, and dynamics necessary to ensure that the crowd acts with wisdom rather than madness.

PART II

Leading a Collaborative Team

Chapter Sixteen

GRAPPLING WITH GROUPTHINK

Alone we can do so little; together we can do so much.
—Helen Keller, author, activist

None of us is as dumb as all of us.
—NASA

ON JANUARY 28, 1986, the space shuttle *Challenger* crashed shortly after takeoff, killing all seven astronauts on board.[1] This event has come to be understood as having been caused in part by groupthink, the phenomenon where social pressure to reach a consensus leads individual members of the group to refrain from expressing their misgivings.[2] After the disaster, the National Aeronautics and Space Administration (NASA) suspended the space shuttle program, and President Ronald Reagan established the Rogers Commission to investigate the accident and its root causes. The technical, engineering explanation for the cause was the failure of the spacecraft's O-rings, which was exacerbated by cold temperatures at the time of the launch. However, the technical explanation is incomplete, as the O-rings had been identified as a risk by NASA engineers as far back as the 1970s, and the risk of cold temperatures had also been discussed as a concern. In the end, it was determined that the organizational structure and culture of NASA, which at that time encouraged conformity and consensus and failed to empower subordinates in the hierarchy, bore at least some of the blame.

Twenty-five years after that tragic event, on January 8, 2011, another tragedy occurred. Astronaut Mark Kelly received a phone call to tell him that his wife, Congresswoman Gabby Giffords, had just been shot outside a grocery store near Tucson, Arizona. He raced to Tucson's University Medical Center, where Giffords was in critical condition. Over the next several days, a team of top surgeons worked to save Giffords's life. At a critical juncture, Kelly was asked to approve a choice between two risky surgery options to remove the bullet from his wife's brain.

Kelly has described the process that he undertook to make this life-or-death decision. He recognized that he was emotionally distraught, sleep deprived, and not in a position to make a wise judgment. He gathered the large group of doctors working on the case into a small break room at the hospital. He looked around the room and identified the most junior member of the team, a young female resident. "Tell me what you would do. I don't want you to tell me what your boss thinks, I want to know what *you* think. What would you do if you were in my shoes?" He then went around the room in reverse order of hierarchy, asking the same question. Recalling the excessive deference to authority at NASA that had led to the disasters of *Challenger* and *Columbia* (a second fatal space shuttle crash that occurred in 2003), Kelly recognized the need to undermine the potential groupthink that could creep in due to the hierarchy within the medical team. He wanted independent perspectives, not one opinion, with all the others falling into line to form a consensus. After listening to the various viewpoints from the doctors, Kelly made his decision, and the surgery was a success.

At NASA, signs are now posted to remind everyone, "None of us is as dumb as all of us."

Not all examples of groupthink involve tragedy. An amusing illustration of conformity was told to me by a sales leader at Goldman Sachs. He found himself riding an elevator with a few of his clients. A short time earlier, they had been discussing cognitive biases, including conformity, so they quickly agreed among themselves to run an experiment. They would each face the wrong way (i.e., facing the back of the elevator) to see what would happen if a stranger got on at the next floor. Sure enough, the new occupant, after a moment of confusion, joined the crowd in their unusual stance.

Researcher Solomon Asch conducted formal conformity experiments in the 1950s. In these experiments, several subjects (all but one of whom were confederates working with Asch) were brought into a room and shown cards (figure 16.1), each with a sample line segment and three lines of varying lengths offered as answer choices. They were asked which of the three lines matched the length of the sample line segment, and, initially, all individuals gave the correct answers. For later answers, the confederates intentionally gave the incorrect answer. In the initial version of the experiment in 1951, the test subject conformed to give the obviously wrong answer 32 percent of the time.[3]

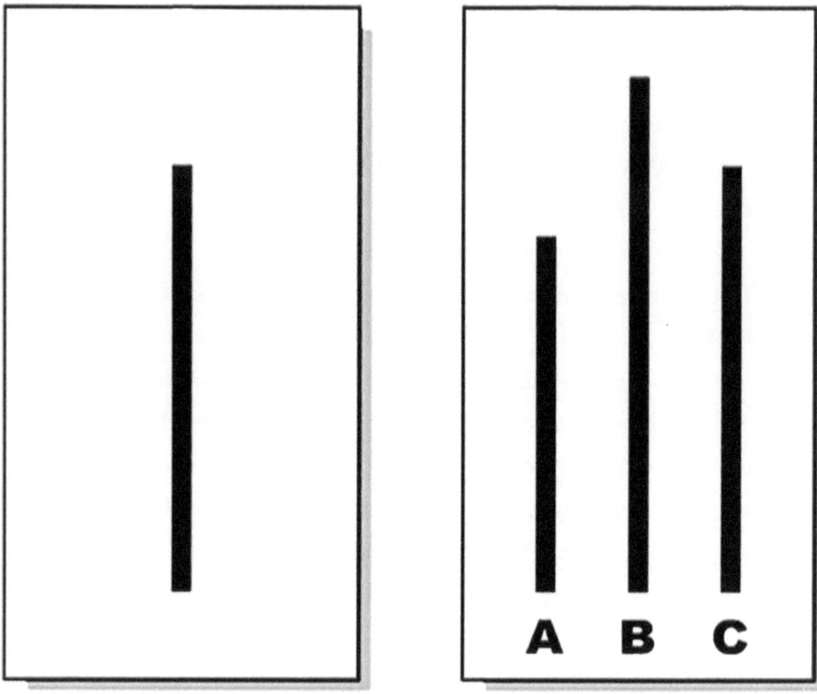

FIGURE 16.1 The Asch experiment: Does line A, B, or C match the line on the first card?

Credit: Fred the Oyster. *Asch experiment*. SVG file. Wikimedia Commons. https://commons.wikimedia.org/wiki/File:Asch_experiment.svg, last modified August 8, 2015.

When the test subjects were later interviewed and asked why they conformed, they gave two reasons. In some cases, the subjects were convinced that they must be wrong, and the majority correct, so they subverted their own judgment. In other cases, the subjects knew that the answer was incorrect but did not want to cause trouble or stand alone against the group.

Interestingly, in later trials, Asch discovered that the level of conformity could be reduced by modifying certain features of the experiment. First, if the group size was small, the conformity percentage went down. If there was only one other (confederate) subject, the wrong answer was matched on just 3 percent of occasions. If there were two, the wrong answer was given 13 percent of the time, and if there were three, the conformity level rose to 32 percent. But beyond three, it rose no further, suggesting that this is the size at which the group dominates the individual in terms of pressure to conform.

Another tweak that made a big difference was adding an ally to the mix. When one of the confederates was instructed to give the correct answer (with the remainder of the group continuing to give the same, incorrect one), the test subject gave the incorrect answer just 5 percent of the time.

Finally, the test subjects also tended to give the correct answer with more frequency if they were told to write it down, away from the prying eyes and peer pressure to which an oral answer would subject them.

Many leaders do not appreciate the impact that their own authority has on the group and conformity. They view themselves as open minded and actively solicit input from subordinates. But they fail to receive productive criticism and opposing perspectives because their junior colleagues do not feel empowered, motivated, or incentivized to speak up. Often the leader is unaware of the subtle incentives that one feels to bite one's tongue or fall in line.

Simple question phrasing can make a big difference. "Am I right?" will solicit different answers from "Where am I wrong?" A leader can ensure that subordinates understand their duty to attempt to poke holes in an idea by conveying humility and uncertainty. You can try saying, "I know that there must be something I am missing here. I would like everyone to give me their two best arguments against moving forward with this proposal." Now, failing to come up with a counterargument in front of peers is a shortcoming rather than a virtue.

This phenomenon can be a particular blind spot for Americans and other Westerners when dealing with colleagues from countries with important cultural differences around hierarchy. Americans tend to be direct, even abrasive communicators and often operate within relatively flat hierarchical structures. Other cultures, particularly those of Asian countries, have communication styles and norms that are indirect, diplomatic, and deferential to authority.

One of my colleagues at Goldman Sachs experienced this phenomenon firsthand. He was a British managing director with an American style of directness who took an expatriate assignment in Tokyo, leading the Japan equity team, which was made up exclusively of Japanese nationals. Before long, he came to view the junior members of his team as more talented than the senior ones. He asked these junior analysts to offer their opinions when potential investment ideas were under discussion. They bit their tongues. He urged, prodded, and begged. Nothing. Exasperated, he asked his own boss, an American, for advice. This was her suggestion: "Have everyone submit a minimum of two questions ahead of time to one of the administrative assistants. Have the administrative assistant collate the questions into a list without attribution so that no one knows who asked which question. Distribute the list 2–3 days before the meeting so that the full team can see the types of questions being asked and the presenter doesn't feel caught off guard."

This simple trick was effective. Given the cover of anonymity and the expectation to contribute, the junior analysts led with their toughest, most probing questions about each new investment idea. It also had the indirect benefit of ensuring that everyone was prepared for the meeting. Performance improved and was soon in the top decile versus competitor funds.

At Eaton Vance, we made extensive use of anonymous questions. We extended the concept to include blind votes. At the end of an investment discussion, we asked all the members of the team to indicate their preference on a scrap of paper, which was folded and collected along with the other votes. This nonbinding vote gave the lead portfolio manager a sense of how much support the idea had and whether further work needed to be undertaken before initiating a position. When the votes were taken by an open show of hands, objections were rare, but with the cover of anonymity, one or two dissents became common. At the Babson College Fund, after a stock is presented to the class, the students and the executives-in-residence vote on the decision online and provide anonymous feedback, which is distributed to everyone the following day.

The benefit of a blind vote is illustrated in the film *12 Angry Men*. The 1957 film tells the story of a jury's deliberation in a murder trial. Shortly after entering the jury room, the group takes an initial vote with a show of hands, which comes out 11–1 in favor of a guilty verdict. Henry Fonda's character, the lone dissenter, is berated by several of the others for being obstinate. Eventually, he gambles by agreeing to a second vote in which he will not participate and whose result he will go along with—if it is a *secret* ballot. A second dissenter emerges from this process.

The shape of the table can also affect jury deliberations. A circular table is thought to be more egalitarian, subtly inviting every juror to participate, whereas a rectangular table is more hierarchical, allowing the jury foreperson to guide the discussion with more authority. The round table has been found to invite more participation at the expense of decisiveness and speed in the decision-making process.

Besides these structural tools designed to undermine hierarchy, there are softer techniques that a leader can use to avoid conformity and seek independent input. They can actively solicit dissent. Publicly compliment and give other visible rewards to those who speak up. To avoid unwanted conformity, leaders should also be wary of tipping off the team as to which way they are leaning. This can be difficult to do, as the agenda of the meeting, topics of discussion, and questions will often give it away. This can be addressed by appointing a deputy to set the agenda and lead the debate. Alternatively, leaders can play devil's advocate to their own predilection to encourage the build-out of the contra case.

SOLUTION SUMMARY

1. **Instill a culture of dissent.** Establish a process of debate. Embrace constructive conflict.
2. **Give subordinates the cover of anonymity.** For example, conduct a blind vote on important questions. For controversial or uncertain discussions, ask that questions be sent ahead of time to a trusted third party to be collated and shared without attribution.
3. **The leader speaks last.** Disguise or delay sharing one's preferred course of action. Solicit opinions from the team either privately or in reverse hierarchical order. This helps to avoid conformity and the "yes man" effect.

Chapter Seventeen

TEAM VERSUS INDIVIDUAL

The madness of crowds.

—Charles Mackay, poet, journalist, and author, 1841

The wisdom of crowds.

—James Surowiecki, journalist and author, 2004

CONNECT 4 is a game whose object is to place four red or black plastic discs in a row, either horizontally, vertically, or diagonally. The outcome is often decided when one of the players overlooks an obvious block of their opponent's winning move.

Several years ago, I attended a social gathering where an oversized, outdoor version of Connect 4 had been set up for play. I wandered over to the game to observe. There were eight players who had divided themselves into two teams of four. I thought, "This is silly. The premise of the game is undermined by playing in groups of four. One person can overlook an obvious move, but there is no way all four teammates will make the same mistake." I was wrong. Midway through the first game, one team made a silly blunder and lost.

Somehow the group had a collective blind spot. Why? Perhaps they were all looking at the board from the same vantage point. Perhaps each of them was treating the game casually, assuming that one of their teammates would catch any mistakes. The consequences of losing a social game of Connect 4 are minor. For more important decisions, though, it is worth asking whether the best outcomes are likely to be achieved by a single individual operating alone or by a collaborative group. Complex decisions involving uncertainty can benefit from a range of perspectives and expertise. However, when a group operates collectively, it can turn into a blind mob where the individuals influence one another in a negative way.[1]

Throughout the history of financial markets, mass hysteria has periodically led to price bubbles that later dramatically burst. One of these, the South Sea Company bubble of 1720, was a British stock mania that financially devastated thousands of people. Even the brilliant physicist Sir Isaac Newton got caught up in the excitement, losing a small fortune, which led him to say, "I can calculate the motion of heavenly bodies, but not the madness of people." The South Sea Company bubble is one of three speculative bubbles discussed by Charles Mackay in *Extraordinary Popular Delusions and the Madness of Crowds*.[2]

Many years later, James Surowiecki argued that—far from being delusional or mad—crowds could be counted on to generate estimates or answers to questions that are more reliable than those provided by a single expert. Surowiecki tells the story of Francis Galton, a British scientist who, in 1906, happened upon a country fair. At the fair, a contest was being held where fairgoers could guess the weight of an ox that was on display. Galton was curious about the collective judgment of the crowd, among whom a handful were livestock experts or farmers, while the majority were laypeople with no expertise.

Given the aggregate makeup of the contestants, he expected the average of their guesses to be wildly off the mark. After getting his hands on the 800 entry forms, he calculated the average guess at 1,197 pounds, just 1 pound less than the correct answer, 1,198 pounds.[3]

Later research found that a select group of diverse perspectives can outperform both the individual and the large crowd. This optimizes between the benefits of diverse opinions and the risk of correlation of errors.[4]

Cliff Asness, a founding principal of the quantitative investment firm AQR Capital Management, took a stab at the answer to the question of when groups are effective decision-making bodies: "'Crowds' are either super-wise or dangerously dumb. The key variable is whether the crowd is made up of independent decision makers (think 'poll the crowd' in Who Wants to Be A Millionaire) or coordinated (think about a mob with pitchforks and torches). Social media, and the internet in general, has made it much easier for coordination to occur. You do the math."[5]

Like Asness, Surowiecki also emphasized the importance of making sure that the crowd or group has members who are acting independently. If, for example, the fairgoers in the ox-weight-estimating experiment had first gathered to compare notes and discuss the matter with one another or had all read the same how-to guide on methods to calculate the weight of livestock, their answers would have been more correlated and the crowd's "wisdom" would have been diminished. In fact, it is not really the "crowd" that has wisdom, but rather the collection of people acting on their own as individuals.

The types of decisions that lend themselves to the benefit of a large group of individual actors are those that require an estimate or forecast or have a factual answer, such as a straightforward pop culture trivia question. In these cases, the group size should be as large as possible.

Decision types that are best handled by a single individual are those that require boldness or bucking of conventional wisdom, such as the one that Abraham Lincoln faced in the introduction. In these cases, the decision maker should collect as much information as possible and solicit input from trusted experts in a setting that avoids groupthink, but ultimately decide on their own.

For highly technical questions that require narrow subject matter expertise where there is an objectively correct answer or approach, I believe that the best decision-making structure is a single, highly qualified expert working with either a checklist or an empowered colleague with equivalent expertise whose mandate is to disagree and find mistakes. Examples of these types of decisions include piloting an aircraft, performing surgery, designing the engineering plans for a bridge, and conducting a scientific experiment. In these cases, a large group of laypeople are unlikely to be helpful, but a qualified individual acting completely alone may be susceptible to errors of omission or oversight.

A fourth category of decisions, and the one with which I have had the most experience in my career, is that where a small group of collaborators is optimal. These decisions involve situations that are complex, nuanced, uncertain, and require well-informed judgments. They benefit from a repeatable approach, with a diverse team of individuals, a supportive culture, and a well-designed process for reaching conclusions.

The typical structure of the investment teams that I have led includes the team leader, a co–portfolio manager (i.e., second-in-command), and several investment analysts. The analysts have responsibility for a specific economic sector that includes several smaller industry groups. For example, an analyst might be the healthcare specialist and is expected to develop expertise and have investment opinions on the stocks of companies in the pharmaceutical, biotechnology, medical device, and health insurance industries. This group of companies might be further constrained by geographic domicile (e.g., only US companies) or market capitalization (e.g., only companies with a market value of more than $10 billion), which would leave a coverage universe of perhaps fifty to seventy-five stocks.

Many firms in the asset management industry run a hierarchical model in which the portfolio manager sits at the top of the organizational chart. This portfolio manager may have dedicated analysts assigned solely to them (a team-based model) or may share a pool of central research analysts with other portfolio managers at the firm. While both models can be successful, I prefer the team-based model. It is more empowering for the analysts because they work closely with their portfolio manager rather than reporting to the director of research. It also leads to better focus and accountability that might otherwise be lacking. Rather than working on a growth stock one day, a value stock the next, and a small-cap stock on the third day, the analyst has a manageable coverage universe, knows the philosophy of the portfolio manager and the client (or fund) guidelines, and can be purposeful in the work.

Portfolio managers often have big egos and are well compensated. They can have tempers and short fuses. Their interaction with an analyst may consist of the analyst nervously "pitching" a new investment "recommendation," while the portfolio managers impatiently listen. Portfolio managers often value "conviction" in the recommendations from their analysts.

The reason why I put those various words from the prior paragraph inside quotation marks is because each one is a pet peeve of mine. Using those words as part of an asset management firm's cultural lexicon leads to detachment and a lack of ownership and accountability on the part of the analyst. The analysts who were members of the teams that I led understood that I wanted to know which stocks they wanted to "own" on behalf of our clients; I was not interested in being "pitched." I did not want a detached "recommendation." The word "conviction" was a particularly bad one in my mind because, in the pursuit of overcoming analysis paralysis and waffling, it put analysts on the spot, forcing them to take a stand, which could lead to various biases later (e.g., endowment effect, sunk-cost fallacy, and confirmation bias) as they dug their heels in to look strong.

The empowered model that I prefer pushes decisions down to the analyst. The logic of this is that the analyst is closest to the individual stock and is likely better positioned to act in a timely, decisive manner. By having an extra layer in the decision-making process, a bias is likely to develop where the analysts who are most articulate or regularly express high confidence find more of their stocks in the portfolio, which is not necessarily a good outcome. A handful of firms in the asset management industry offer analyst-run funds where the analysts have full discretion to buy and sell stocks within their area of coverage responsibility. These funds are often high-performing, but have minimal assets invested in them, because they tend to have a higher number of holdings and there is no one dominant person in charge, both of which are features that clients and their consultants tend not to like.

In the empowered model, the leader still has an important role to play. I think of the leader of an empowered investment team as having a similar role to that of an orchestra's conductor. The conductor has the responsibility of selecting the music that will be played, choosing the musicians who will fill the seats, and ensuring that the collective output is harmonious. The conductor plays the orchestra the way that an individual musician plays their instrument. The investment leader sets the philosophy and strategy for the investment portfolio, establishing risk parameters and ensuring that those controls are followed. Also, cash tends to rise and fall as investment positions come and go, so managing the cash level to minimize "cash drag" requires a central authority.[6] They can also encourage analysts to work on certain new opportunities or themes and will also lead the discussion/debate within the team. The proverbial buck stops with the leader.

In any organization, there is natural tension between distributing authority versus maintaining central control at a higher level. Each approach has its pros and cons. The empowered model can be nimbler and puts the decisions in the hands of those with the most direct expertise and current information. It also typically increases job satisfaction for those who have been given discretion to perform their duties. The central control model has the advantage of keeping interrelated decisions coordinated and consistent. Also, the individuals who make up central command are typically more senior, have more experience, and have a high-level perspective (i.e., being able to "see the forest for the trees"). In a military campaign, for example, feedback from the front lines is important, but so is a full understanding of the battlefield, including knowledge of other assets that are available to be deployed.

SOLUTION SUMMARY

1. **Identify the decision type.** Adapt the size of the decision-making unit to the task at hand.
2. **Use polls when data is dispersed.** The larger the group size, the better. Viewpoints must be independent of one another.
3. **Experts are best for technical tasks.** Empower the specialist, but also ensure that oversight is provided via a checklist or devil's advocate.

Chapter Eighteen

IDEAL TEAM SIZE

Two heads are better than one.

—Proverb noted by writer John Heywood, 1546

Too many cooks spoil the broth.

—Proverb noted by historian John Hooker, 1575

IF YOU were planning to throw a dinner party and were eager for the group to engage deeply on a topic such that a single conversation would be maintained, how many people would you invite?

Over the years, there have been various attempts to calculate or observe the optimal number of people in a group:

- The "dinner party problem" is the notion that if there are more than four people at a dinner party, the conversation will naturally splinter into multiple conversations. Potential reasons for this constraint include limits of cognition (maintaining an understanding of each person's perspective), limits on the mind's ability to process information, and simply the difficulty in hearing the conversation as the group size grows.[1]
- British anthropologist Robin Dunbar studied nonhuman primates to develop the theory that the maximum

sustainable size of a social group is related to the ratio of the size of the brain's neocortex to the body. For humans, this suggested the "Dunbar number" of 150 meaningful social connections that can be maintained at any one time. Dunbar observed that deeper relationships require a smaller subset: 50 for "friends," 15 for "good friends," and 5 for "loved ones."[2]

- Bain & Company argues that once you reach seven individuals in a decision-making group, the effectiveness of the group's decisions will be reduced by 10 percent for each new member added to the team.[3] As team size grows, diminishing returns can set in.
- Summarizing the research on optimal team size in a business setting, Jaime Potter, a talent recruiter formerly of McKinsey & Company, wrote:

> Across these studies, the exact answer varies depending on the exact task, but the modal answer is 3–5 people. In a seminal book on the topic, Ivan Steiner arrives at about five to six people, with the answer varying slightly depending on the exact task. More recently, the late Patrick Laughlin performed a controlled laboratory experiment . . . In this experiment, the task being completed was a "letters-to-numbers problem," a type of puzzle where teams must learn the predetermined mapping of 10 letters to 10 numbers as quickly as possible. Notably, this task has a dominant strategy that, once discovered, leads to the quickest unveiling of the solution. The ideal team size in this case? Just three.[4]

So the optimal decision-making unit can be as few as three people, and it is likely no more than four or five.

One of the equity investment teams at an Eaton Vance affiliate had just three individuals. This team was highly successful in terms of both its performance record and its ability to attract clients. They were able to accomplish this by minimizing the number of different products (i.e., focusing on funds or portfolios with only small and midsized US domiciled companies); being strict about their investment criteria, which eliminated certain swaths of the market; keeping the number of holdings per portfolio down (typically fewer than fifty positions); and maintaining low churn or turnover (so there was not a frequent need for new investment ideas).

The investment teams that I have personally led have been somewhat larger, having typically six to ten investors. This has been a function of the desire to maintain coverage of all economic sectors, with specialized expertise in each sector. Standard & Poor's and MSCI maintain eleven Global Industry Classification Standard (GICS) sectors: energy, materials, industrials, consumer discretionary, consumer staples, health care, financials, information technology, communication services, utilities, and real estate. Depending on the depth and breadth of analyst coverage desired, an individual can potentially take responsibility for more than one sector. Specifically, energy and materials naturally go together since both are highly sensitive to commodity prices; consumer staples and consumer discretionary can also go together for obvious reasons.

Since the size of the teams that I led were already above the ideal number, I was ruthless about limiting the attendees at our weekly investment meetings, where we would debate existing holdings and new ideas in depth. Despite the dry nature of the subject matter, there always seemed to be someone who wanted to join the meeting. We had institutional/client portfolio managers (IPM/CPM), whose job was to be embedded in the investment team so they could communicate effectively with clients. We had summer interns who understandably wanted exposure to the investment process and senior investors. We had analysts from adjacent investment teams who covered the companies being discussed at a particular meeting. We also received invitation requests from our salespeople, who wanted to join so they could purportedly be more credible when pitching our products to prospective clients. I regularly said no to this last group since I believed their attendance would create the equivalent of the "observer effect" in quantum mechanics, where observation by a detector or instrument can change the results of an experiment.

Debate and disagreement were part of these investment teams' ethos, so it was important that individuals on the team knew and trusted one another. I did not want team members to pull punches or feel the need to "put on a show" for an audience.

When I first arrived at Eaton Vance, one of the complaints that I heard was about the ineffectiveness of a weekly meeting called "Fresh Money Thursdays." These meetings were well intentioned. They were held in a large conference room with a projection screen. It was a lunchtime meeting, so attendees were invited to bring their lunches. Staff from outside the department were included and regularly attended these meetings. Typically, twenty-five to thirty-five people were in the room.

The analyst walked through a lengthy Microsoft PowerPoint presentation and then fielded questions. These questions were nearly always softballs because no one wanted to show up a colleague in front of such a large, less familiar audience. We disbanded these meetings shortly after my arrival and conducted investment meetings in smaller group sizes with a streamlined set of materials. The debates became more animated and probing, leading to better investment decisions.

The advent of video conferencing has become a new challenge for the leader who wishes to maintain a small, effective working group. The link to the meeting can be forwarded internally, and the threshold for "dropping in" can be low. One never quite knows who might be listening in, which restrains candor. In my opinion, the least effective meetings are the so-called hybrid ones, where certain individuals are in the room and others are on video. Sometimes colleagues who are in the building still elect to conference in rather than show up. To address this problem, I have seen a few managers remove video as an option; either come to the meeting in person or not at all.

One of the ways in which leaders become leaders is through their personal extroversion. Earlier in their careers, they may have been more vocal. Their networking skills may also have been strong. If they assume others are like themselves, they may miss important insights from introverted individuals who feel uncomfortable speaking in a group setting. In my observation, the role of buy-side analyst attracts a disproportionate share of introverts. Making an effort to seek out the opinions of these quieter individuals can ensure that good ideas are not overlooked.

SOLUTION SUMMARY

1. **Go for Goldilocks group size.** Groups should be large enough to have breadth of perspective but small enough to avoid bureaucracy. The ideal size can be as few as three to five individuals.
2. **Meetings are invitation only.** Particularly if sensitive or controversial topics are under discussion, extra bodies around the table (or faces on the screen) can lead to valuable perspectives not being aired.
3. **Engage introverts one-on-one.** Recognize that certain individuals prefer not to speak up in front of a large group.

Chapter Nineteen

BUILDING THE TEAM

There's no "I" in team.

—Shaquille O'Neal, former NBA player

There's a "M-E."

—Kobe Bryant, former NBA player (as retold by Shaquille O'Neal)

APRIL 12, 2008, was a life-changing day for me. Midafternoon on Saturday, I was watching the Masters golf tournament on the television in my New York City apartment. My mobile phone rang. It was my boss from Goldman Sachs.

"Eddie, I am in London right now. Our chief investment officer of European Equity has resigned. I think you would be perfect for the job. Can you get on a plane to London tomorrow?"

I did get on a flight the next day, and by the end of the day on Monday, I had decided to relocate my young family for an expatriate assignment of unknown length. The combination of excitement and jet lag made it impossible to sleep that week. I decided to fully embrace the new assignment immediately by quickly wrapping things up in my old role and moving into a corporate apartment in London the following week.

The next six months were the most difficult of my life. I had several overlapping objectives. I had to immediately shore up the business by meeting with clients to reassure them that their money was in a safe pair of hands. I needed to learn the portfolio of European stocks that I had inherited from my predecessor; most of these companies were unfamiliar to me. I had to study for, and take, the UK securities regulation exam, which had different principles and terminology from what I was used to under US regulations. On the personal front, I needed to find a permanent place to live, cancel my lease back in New York, arrange for an international move of our belongings, speak with an immigration attorney, open a UK bank account, and even more. Oh, and all of this was happening against the backdrop of a rapidly unfolding global financial crisis while I was working for one of the firms at the center of all the commotion.

While my arrival at the Goldman Sachs London office was an exciting development in my own career, a few of my new colleagues did not share my enthusiasm. From their perspective, the powers that be back at the New York headquarters had parachuted in one of their own to show the locals how to do their jobs, and this new guy was not even capable of correctly pronouncing the names of certain European companies held in the portfolios.

These new colleagues quickly divided themselves into three groups. The first took a wait-and-see approach. They expressed some trepidation at the change but otherwise did what they were asked. A second, small group decided to embrace my arrival. They seemed to say to themselves, "Yes, there may be a lot of uncertainty, but this guy was chosen for a reason, and if we take a positive view and work to support him, maybe opportunities will present themselves later." The third group resisted my arrival. This took the form of snide remarks and muffled giggles, as well as closed-door meetings to discuss the shortcomings of the new boss.

At the time, I had the title of vice president, which was below that of managing director, the title carried by two British employees who were now reporting to me. I would not be eligible for the coveted "managing director" title until the end of the year. In title-conscious Great Britain, this created an awkward dynamic for me and undermined my authority.

As I struggled to deal with the subordinates who were resistant, I reflected on a course on the topics of leadership and instituting organizational change that I had taken a few years earlier while at business school. In that course, we discussed a Harvard Business School case study that looked at the challenges faced by Charlotte Beers upon becoming CEO of Ogilvy & Mather Worldwide (O&M), a large, multinational advertising agency that had never had a leader from the outside before. The written case described the situation as follows:

> Beers's appointment, recalled O&M veterans, created initial apprehension. Commented one executive, "She was from a smaller agency in Chicago and had not managed multiple offices. O&M is a worldwide company, and she had never worked outside the United States. And, she was not from Ogilvy." Added another, "This is an organization that rejects outsiders."
>
> Her approach quickly made an impression with Ogilvy insiders. "It was clear from day one that Charlotte would be a different kind of leader. Full of life. Eyes open and clearly

> proud of the brand she was now to lead. Here was somebody who could look around and see the risks, but wasn't afraid to turn the corner even though it was dark out," said one executive. "We had leaders before, who said all the right things, were terribly nice, did a good job, but they didn't inspire. Charlotte has an ability to inspire—Charlotte has presence." Commented another executive, "She is delightfully informal, but you always know that she means business." Within two months of her appointment, Beers dismissed a top-level executive who had failed to instigate necessary changes.[1]

My recollection from the class discussion was that our professor dwelled on this last point for some time. I'm paraphrasing from memory, but he basically said, "What do you do when you have a key lieutenant who is resisting your vision and plan, and the troops are looking on to see how you will deal with it? . . . You need to perform a public hanging." The phrase "public hanging" is so vivid that it has stuck with me. To establish one's authority in the early days of a new assignment, it needs to be made clear throughout the organization that there is only one path forward. This is the metaphorical equivalent of Hernán Cortés scuttling his ships upon arrival in the New World.

In my own situation in London, there was a strong desire to limit personnel turnover. Historically, there was high turnover in the London office, and the client base was thought to be hypersensitive to any further changes. In my initial round of client meetings, I had emphasized continuity of personnel and process, essentially tying my own hands and limiting myself.

On September 15, 2008, Lehman Brothers filed for bankruptcy. Global stock prices, particularly in the financial sector, had already fallen in price and become extremely volatile, but this event took things to a new level, with rapid and unprecedented moves by regulators, central banks, and other actors. Six days later, Goldman Sachs became a bank holding company. Two days after that, the firm received an investment from Warren Buffett, which helped shore up confidence in the firm.[2]

As the fourth quarter of 2008 unfolded, markets remained volatile and fears of a global recession were rampant. Word came down to me that the firm was looking to reduce head count. In the end, we parted ways with two individuals and reassigned responsibilities throughout the investment team. Complaints were muffled, as those who stayed on were thankful to still have their jobs.

The experience of inheriting an existing team is a common one for a manager in a new role. If one is lucky, the mandate may include the opportunity to make a change or two. It is rare that a leader can rebuild a team completely or create a new one from scratch. In the asset management business, where existing clients and their investment consultants abhor change, one is often encouraged to move gradually. In my experience and observations, managers often use this preference for stability to defer addressing difficult personnel decisions and avoid conflict. It is rarely a mistake to move quickly and decisively, particularly at the start, when the mandate for change is fresh.

Whether building a new team or adding to an existing group, it is helpful to seek out people with different skill sets, experiences, and perspectives. If each member of a small team views the world through an identical lens and tackles problems using the same tools, productive disagreement may be rare. One way to accomplish this in the hiring process is to ensure that the interviewers themselves have a range of perspectives and backgrounds.

I have conducted several hundred job interviews. When reviewing the feedback of other interviewers, I often saw the phrase "good cultural fit" as one of the reasons to hire a particular candidate. I came to view this attribute with caution. Obviously, it is good if a prospective hire shares the values of the broader organization, but if "good cultural fit" was a synonym for "just like us," then I worried that we were building a team that would be susceptible to groupthink rather than healthy conflict and original thought.

The feedback from interviewers should be collected immediately. This is best done by having an HR representative (or another similarly detached individual) collect the feedback. It is a mistake to compare notes before embryonic thoughts and reactions have been written down. To do so is to engage in an attempt to find consensus, which can stifle disagreement and mute concerns that should be aired.

Having a standard feedback form with a rating scale can be useful, but the right characteristics need to be on the list. I recall one time when we were interviewing MBA students for an investment analyst position. Since we were looking at a dozen candidates and wanted to bring a semblance of order and objectivity to the decision, a questionnaire had been drafted where the various interviewers were asked to score each interview candidate from 1 to 5 on several metrics. There were two attributes missing from the draft list that I insisted on adding: curiosity and independence of thought. Without those two attributes, the analyst would struggle to outperform the market and would not be a good fit for an investment team that prized professional disagreement and collaborative conflict in the pursuit of world-class investment results for clients.

It can be difficult to assess a person's natural level of curiosity and independence of thought in a thirty-minute interview. I would listen for examples of the candidate bucking the conventional wisdom or engaging in an original pursuit. This might be as simple as asking questions about an unusual hobby in the "personal interests" section of the résumé. Along similar lines, I have worked with other hiring managers in the asset management industry who preferred not to hire individuals who had worked at dot-com start-ups in the late 1990s and early 2000s, spent time in investment banking training programs, or worked in private equity in more recent years. Each of these backgrounds would seem to suggest intelligence, an analytical mindset, and relevant work experience, and often came with an Ivy League diploma to boot. However, this background also suggested individuals who made the popular choice at the time and had demonstrated no passion about being a contrarian stock picker, eager to find ways to beat the market.

To be a successful investor, one needs to be at least a little bit contrarian. If one's opinion on a stock is identical to that of the market, there is no opportunity to be had. Even in the cases where an investor is attracted to a high-flying growth stock that has performed well and is very popular, by making a purchase (or continuing to hold an existing position), the investor is essentially saying, "I know this opportunity is not undiscovered at this point, but the market price of the stock implies that the company's future opportunities are still not sufficiently appreciated." This is its own form of contrarian sentiment.

Early in the film *The Wolf of Wall Street*, Matthew McConaughey asks Leonardo DiCaprio, "Now, did you really pitch a stock in your job interview?"[3] Granted, this is a movie's exaggerated look at Wall Street from a different era and the job is one of commissioned stockbroker rather than buy-side equity analyst, but I find the movie's line of dialogue odd because in asset management, the stock pitch is a standard part of every interview. Candidates know to expect it. The stock pitch is a form of test. The first part of the test is whether the individual knows enough to expect the question; applicants would be rejected if they did not. The second part of the test is how much effort the person has put into preparing the idea. At minimum, candidates should know the company's core business, profitability metrics such as return on invested capital (ROIC), return on equity (ROE), and profit margin; valuation metrics such as price-to-earnings (P/E) ratio, enterprise value/earnings before interest, taxes, depreciation, and amortization (EV/EBITDA), and price-to-book (P/B) ratio, if relevant; and balance sheet metrics such as debt/capital and debt/EBITDA.

The interview candidate should also have a thesis on why the stock can outperform, which is usually some version of what hedge fund manager Michael Steinhardt has referred to as a "variant perception." Variant perception is the important idea that if one's perception of the stock does not vary from that of the market consensus, then there is no opportunity. One must see something different that is not reflected in the current price in order for an opportunity to exist.

Another part of the stock pitch test is how well the candidates field questions from the interviewers. Do they stand their ground when pushed but also concede good counterarguments? Do they admit when they do not know the answer to a question (but also pivot to a "best guess" based on what they do know)? Interviewees should also have at least three different stock pitches prepared in case an interviewer asks for a second one, or if multiple interviewers each ask for a favorite stock (as it is not good to have the interviewers find out later that a candidate used the same stock pitch in each meeting).

Since the stock pitch question is so well anticipated, it tends to be a measure of a candidate's preparation and resourcefulness. To see how well the candidate works under deadline pressure, some firms will assign a stock to an individual and ask the person to spend a week working on it and then present the investment case to a small committee at the hiring firm. I was on the receiving end of this test at Fidelity when trying to land a summer associate internship while attending business school. I was assigned Amdocs, a telecommunications company, and I had only seven days to work on it while I was managing a heavy courseload at school. From my conversations with people who knew the hiring managers at Fidelity, I knew that they were looking for candidates to demonstrate that they had prioritized the assignment by putting in at least twenty hours. Also, I needed to show a piece of original research. Finally, I knew that it was important for me to take a firm stand on the stock, whether for or against.

After doing the obvious things like reading the company's annual report and building a simple valuation model, I decided to call Electronic Data Systems (EDS), a competitor of Amdocs in certain product areas. I knew that it would be difficult to get anyone from management on the phone, but the investor relations representative was happy to chat once I dropped the Fidelity name and told her that I might be working there soon.

The stock appeared very expensive to me, so on the day of the interview, I led off with, "Amdocs is a telecommunications software and services company with attractive growth prospects but, based on its current valuation, the stock is a sell." Later in the conversation, I let it drop that I had spoken with a competitor firm during my due diligence. I literally saw one of the interviewer's eyebrows rise, and I knew that I was in good shape. A couple of days later, I was offered the role.

While these prepared presentations have their place, in my opinion there is no substitute for a stock test that requires candidates to think on their feet. At Goldman Sachs and Eaton Vance, once we reached the final round of interviews for a candidate, we would give the candidate an annual report of our choosing (usually an unfamiliar company with a straightforward business model, but where there was something atypical in the financial statements). The interviewee also received a calculator and the current stock price. They had ninety minutes to form an opinion. By limiting the time and resources, we were able to assess how well the applicants worked under pressure, their strengths or weaknesses in terms of time management, and whether they had the inner confidence to express an opinion on the stock.

It was striking how often this test derailed an otherwise attractive candidate. For example, a person who had been through two or three rounds of interviews, offered polished stock pitches, and seemed strong in all respects would fail to do any valuation work at all on the test stock. In other cases, they would miss a basic accounting principle, such as a mismatch between earnings and cash flow, or they would hem and haw, refusing to say "buy" or "sell" even when prodded.

I believe that some form of test should be used when hiring for virtually any position. For example, my father, a small businessman, used to administer short spelling and arithmetic tests when hiring administrative assistants. An appropriate test can be designed by a hiring manager (in consultation with the HR department to avoid potential legal and regulatory violations). Simply write the two or three success attributes that are difficult to assess subjectively and build a written or physical test to find out about those.

One of the fixed-income teams at Eaton Vance, when hiring junior traders or portfolio assistants, administered a test that, among other things, required candidates to identify erroneously transposed digits in a series of lengthy numbers. My group adopted this test when we were hiring for similar positions where detail orientation was extremely important. Our data science team adopted a short test that required the candidate to write a few lines of code or spot errors in a series of code. It was striking how often individuals who claimed to be experienced software programmers came up short on this test.

In summary, when interviewing prospective hires, it is too easy to over-rely on one's subjective judgment based on listening to prepared answers to a handful of generic interview questions. Supplementing the standard interview with some form of assessment of an individual's skills that are applicable to the job under consideration can be revealing.

SOLUTION SUMMARY

1. **Be decisive during the honeymoon.** A manager in a new role should move quickly when making personnel decisions and introducing new processes. In the early days, change is expected. Take advantage of that. If necessary, perform a public hanging.
2. **Don't compare notes.** Interviewers should submit feedback independently to a detached, objective party like an HR representative so opinions remain independent.
3. **Use tests for hiring.** A test designed to evaluate the skills required by the position is an objective assessment that can be used to supplement the subjective assessment of a conventional interview.

Chapter Twenty

TEAM CULTURE

To get along, you have to go along.
—Sam Rayburn, speaker of the US House of Representatives, 1949–1953

You can disagree without being disagreeable.
—Ruth Bader Ginsburg, Supreme Court justice, 1993–2020

"DARE TO DISAGREE" is a wonderful TED Talk by Margaret Heffernan.[1] The twelve-minute speech has nearly five million views, several of which are mine. Heffernan relates the compelling story of Alice Stewart, a British cancer researcher in the 1950s who discovered that childhood cancer was linked to X-rays of pregnant women, even when the radiation levels were low. The British and American medical establishments were reluctant to embrace the findings, and it took twenty-five years for the practice of using X-ray machines on pregnant women to be discontinued. Heffernan uses this story as a jumping-off point to describe Stewart's working methods.

Stewart had a partner named George Neal, who was a statistician. According to Heffernan, Neal once said, "My job is to prove Dr. Stewart wrong." Heffernan describes this as having a model of collaboration and an approach that actively seeks disconfirmation by intentionally creating conflict.

It is difficult enough to maintain a healthy working relationship built around productive conflict between two people, but as the size of the group grows, it becomes even harder. This is another argument for keeping the team size small.

At the level of the individual, a person's personal character, moral code, values, and personal attributes guide choices and actions. When we interact with others in pursuit of a common goal, our individual attributes and relationships form a culture. The culture of the group is made of a sense of purpose, along with the methods and behaviors employed in pursuit of that purpose. Finite resources, including time, force trade-offs between otherwise noble attributes. For example, if a company has the north star of being first to market with a new product, then quality may suffer. If manufacturing the highest-quality products is the goal, then speed to market may suffer. Culture helps sort these priorities.

When individuals join a group with a strong and clear culture, they typically must assimilate or be rejected. If two groups with differing cultures come together, the situation can feel very disruptive and uncomfortable until a new, integrated culture reveals itself. Organizations often have competing values.[2]

The cultures of financial services firms can differ meaningfully from one another. At the risk of reinforcing stereotypes, here are a few examples: Small community banks and insurance companies can be conservative and risk averse. Large, universal banks can be bureaucratic and regulatory-focused. Hedge funds can be aggressive and brash. Brokerage firms can be short term– and transaction-oriented. Asset management firms, when they are at their best, have a strong investment culture focused on their fiduciary duty to their clients.

Many consultants, sophisticated institutional clients, and other industry observers are skeptical of the ownership model where an asset management firm is the subsidiary of a larger, diversified financial services company. They correctly observe that the parent firm has its own culture that is unlikely to be a fiduciary one. Furthermore, it is rare that the CEO of the parent firm rose through the ranks of the asset management subsidiary, so they may not appreciate this dynamic.

The diversified financial services ownership model can be effective if the asset management subsidiary is allowed to maintain an independent culture and healthy degree of autonomy. I once heard the head of investor relations at a global financial services firm describe staff rotation as one of the benefits of the diversified model: "If we don't have a current job opening for one of our talented investment banking associates, we can just move them into asset management." To someone who has dedicated their career to the fiduciary role of managing clients' money, this sounds like nails on a chalkboard.

One day, during my internship at Fidelity, one of the firm's internal recruiters took the five MBA interns on a brief tour of one of the firm's other Boston buildings, where operational, administrative, and other "back office" matters were handled. While there, she made a statement that has stuck with me: "Everyone who works in these support functions understands that we are an investment firm, and that back in the other building, where you guys are sitting for the summer, that's where the rock stars are." At first blush, I liked the idea that I had the opportunity to become one of the "rock stars," even as I recognized that the statement was a bit obnoxious and dismissive of people who played other important roles at the firm. But it also drove home a critical point: The culture of the firm was driven by the desire to deliver outstanding investment results for clients.

At Eaton Vance, senior leadership emphasized the firm's investment culture by holding the Chartered Financial Analyst® (CFA®) designation in high esteem. The CFA program is a multiyear, self-study program with three separate exams that have high fail rates. Passing all three levels of the CFA is viewed by many in the asset management industry, including myself, as a significant achievement and a statement of dedication and commitment to investing as a career choice. Hanging on the walls of the internal staircase at Eaton Vance was a framed copy of the CFA charter of each person at the firm who carried the designation. This display of charters ran for several floors, and one walked past them on the way to the company cafeteria. They were arranged based on the date that the charter was earned, with the oldest charters on the highest floors. Once a year, the charters had to be rehung from top to bottom to make allowance for employees who had joined or left the firm, as well as new charter holders who had passed Level III of the exam in the past year. In addition to this visible display, an annual CFA luncheon, hosted by the firm's CEO, was held for employees (and their managers) who had passed one of the levels. Further, managers were encouraged to give their employees support during the period leading up to the exam, and once someone had earned the charter, the firm reimbursed the person's annual dues. We were all in on the CFA program as part of the culture, and as a statement, we viewed ourselves as investors first and foremost.

In my experience, business leaders enjoy talking about corporate culture and often make it part of their stump speeches. I have found it to be the case that these leaders will discuss the importance of culture and how strong their own firm's culture is. It is also important to personally model the culture through action and to explain (particularly to new joiners and junior colleagues) how the culture manifests itself in day-to-day activities. Incentives should also be aligned to reinforce the culture.

For a team or organization that desires to have a culture of healthy conflict, hiring individuals who are original thinkers comes first. The next step is to create a team dynamic that encourages disagreement. It is not enough for the team leader just to say, "I would like for our group to challenge one another and highlight the shortcomings of ideas that are proposed. Let's try to prove each other wrong." This mindset needs to be embedded in the team's ethos or culture. It does not come easily for most people to engage in conflict, even if it is productive. Individuals often feel like they are being rude or unnecessarily provocative. They are rocking the boat and disturbing the peace.

SOLUTION SUMMARY

1. **Lead by example.** To establish and maintain a strong culture, walk the walk.
2. **Use repetition and visual cues.** A leader's stump speech should become so familiar that members of the organization can recite it by rote. Visual symbols are subtle daily reminders of the organization's priorities.
3. **Reinforce culture through incentives.** Such incentives can be direct financial rewards or recognition through public praise, opportunities for new assignments, or promotions.

Chapter Twenty One

MENTAL MODELS

Give me a place to stand and a lever long enough, and I will move the world.

—Archimedes, Greek mathematician, third century BCE

To a man with a hammer everything looks like a nail.

—Abraham Maslow, psychologist, 1966

IN 1939, at an English country estate named Bletchley Park, a shy genius named Alan Turing led a band of misfits in an attempt to break Nazi Germany's Enigma machine, which was used to send encrypted messages to conduct its war effort. The code was believed to be unbreakable due to its complex system of rotors and keys that changed daily.

At its peak, Bletchley Park operated twenty-four hours a day and employed around 10,000 people, roughly 75 percent of whom were women. Turing's team recruited experts from a wide range of areas. These included mathematicians, linguists, engineers, translators, chess players, and even crossword puzzle enthusiasts. On January 13, 1942, they quietly placed a cryptic crossword in the *Daily Telegraph* and asked members of the public who were able to solve it in under twelve minutes to write in to the newspaper. The team covertly approached this group and ultimately recruited several of them to work at Bletchley Park.[1]

Turing and his team built an electromechanical device called Bombe, which could rapidly test thousands of possible Enigma settings. In addition to breaking Enigma, Bletchley Park's personnel were able to break Lorenz, a cipher used by Adolf Hitler for his personal messages. These achievements likely helped bring an earlier end to World War II in Europe.

An important theme of this book has been the shortcoming of *heuristics*, mental shortcuts or rules of thumb that we all use in everyday life. A more sophisticated sounding term is *mental model*, a way of viewing the world or a situation. It is a perspective drawn from knowledge and experience.

When tackling linear, straightforward problems, mental models can be very useful. When deployed against nuanced or complex ones, they can be insufficient, or even counterproductive. Cognitive biases arise when we over-rely on a singular framework. This is the key idea behind Daniel Kahneman's system 1 and system 2 thinking.

In chapter 19, we discussed the value of having cognitive diversity within a team. Different experiences and perspectives can cover blind spots and bring fresh ideas to tackle a stale problem. The successes at Bletchley Park are great examples of the benefits of putting together an unorthodox team of individuals with different strengths and perspectives.

For individuals operating alone, developing a range of expertise and perspectives will help them become deeper thinkers and better decision makers. Rather than relying on a single framework to tackle the problem, Charlie Munger, who was Warren Buffett's long-time partner and confidant, advised using a "latticework of mental models" from different disciplines.[2]

Shane Parrish, who writes the excellent *Farnum Street* blog and hosts a podcast by the same name, has collated approximately 100 mental models that come from the worlds of economics, psychology, chemistry, physics, biology, and more.[3] What follows is a partial list of the models that Parrish has identified, along with my explanation of its connection to investing:

- **Circle of competence:** Invest in what you know.
- **Second-order thinking:** Sometimes the inverse conclusion is correct. Stocks can go up on bad news when the bad news is already more than discounted in the price.
- **Probabilistic thinking:** This idea is discussed throughout this book, along with concepts like the multiverse and probability-weighted price targets.
- **Inertia:** Momentum in security prices is a documented phenomenon.
- **Leverage:** This concept includes financial leverage, operating leverage, and leveraging knowledge and resources to create scale.
- **Catalysts:** The best catalysts for stock prices are ones that are not immediately visible and therefore are not already factored into the price.
- **Ecosystems:** The 2020–2021 global supply chain disruptions are a good example of the importance of ecosystems.
- **Hierarchical organization:** In chapter 16, we discussed the risks of having too much hierarchy in a team's decision process.
- **Feedback loops:** Feedback loops can be positive or negative. Great companies often have a "flywheel effect," in

which success begets success through scale and natural monopolies.

- **Margin of safety:** This is Ben Graham's core concept.
- **Algorithms:** Electronic trading.
- **Trade-offs:** Time and money are finite resources that must be allocated efficiently.
- **Social proof:** Many investors are reluctant to go against the consensus and take comfort when others agree with them.

SOLUTION SUMMARY

1. **Go a mile wide and a few inches deep.** Expose yourself to a range of disciplines and make sure that you understand the core concepts of each. Apply them in your own domains.
2. **Avoid over-relying on a single model.** Frameworks and heuristics are useful in moderation but can become biases when overused.
3. **Use a latticework of mental models.** When tackling a complex problem, take Charlie Munger's advice and utilize a range of perspectives and approaches.

Chapter Twenty Two

INCENTIVES

It is not from the benevolence of the butcher, the brewer, or the baker that we expect our dinner, but from their regard to their own interest.

~ Adam Smith, *Wealth of Nations*, 1776

What gets measured gets managed.

~ Peter Drucker, paraphrased from *The Practice of Management*, 1954

EXASPERATION WAS the best word to capture how Ella was feeling. The clutter her son, Grant, left in his bedroom and around the house had become too much. The bed was never made. The carpet was not visible due to a layer of dirty clothes, wet towels, and sports equipment. No amount of yelling, cajoling, nagging, or reprimanding led to sustained compliance with her wishes for a tidy house.

In desperation, the mother decided to implement a monetary reward scheme. She would pay her son $10 per hour to clean up. He was eager for the money, so he happily agreed to the arrangement. After a couple of weeks, though, Ella found herself paying a small fortune for the work. When she observed Grant "working," he was moving at a snail's pace, checking his phone constantly, and taking frequent breaks, all the while racking up billable hours.

The innovative mother decided to reorient the payment plan so it would be based on volume rather than time. She would pay twenty-five cents for each article of clothing, ball, or other item that was put in its proper place. In the first week of this new system, it was highly effective. Her son's energy level went up as he rushed through the house completing his chores. However, in the second week, the house was messier than ever. She noticed more clothes on the floor, including ones that Grant had not even worn. It became apparent that the clever mom had an equally clever son, who emptied everything out of his dresser and closet just so he would have something to pick up later. He had also poured a basket of tennis balls on the floor and was counting each ball as a twenty-five-cent item. The bill went back up—and the mess grew, too.

Poorly designed incentive programs can fail to produce intended results or, worse, produce the opposite. Whether in a personal setting or in the business world, perverse incentives can be costly. An important leadership responsibility is designing and implementing an effective incentive system for the team.

As an investor, I followed the US banking sector from 2003–2007. I saw the management of Wells Fargo present to an audience of professional investors on several occasions. They had a standard stump speech and slide presentation, in which they emphasized the higher profitability of their customers who had multiple accounts with the bank. At that time, alongside Jamie Dimon's JP Morgan Chase, Wells Fargo was regarded as one of the best two large banks in the United States. Wells Fargo shares were valued by the market at a premium to other banks. Like JP Morgan, the company weathered the 2008 financial crisis relatively well.

Several years later, on September 8, 2016, it came to light that Wells Fargo employees had opened at least 2 million unauthorized customer accounts. The bank was initially fined $185 million. Twelve days later, the CEO, John Stumpf, was dragged in front of the US Congress to face tough questions; he would leave the company a month later.

It was revealed that the bank had attempted to drive the goal of having more accounts per customer with a series of financial incentives designed to encourage employees to cross-sell the bank's products. The bank used the term "Going for Gr-Eight" to emphasize the goal of having at least eight products for each customer. Employees had quotas and sales goals oriented around cross-selling. In the extreme, employees who missed these targets could lose their jobs.

In the year after the scandal broke, it came to light that there was a total of 3.5 million phony accounts. Between 2018 and 2025, Wells Fargo was required by its regulator, the Federal Reserve, to operate under an asset cap, which had the effect of limiting its growth and earnings. Over that period, the bank paid fines, settlements, and refunds to various entities, which summed up to more than $9 billion. The cost of its faulty incentive system was steep.

When financial incentives are modest in size, they can backfire. In one study, parents who were fined for picking up their children late from daycare simply treated the fine as an additional price to be paid, and late pickups increased.[1]

The topic of incentives is well trodden.[2] I will focus on my experience developing incentive plans for investment personnel in the asset management industry. The typical pay structure for investment staff consists of a base salary and an annual bonus. The bonus is often made up of cash and a deferred equity component. For senior employees and those performing at a high level, bonuses can be multiples of the base pay. In addition to the obvious monetary incentives, I have found employees to be motivated by job title, level of responsibility, and recognition.

Certain asset management firms use formulaic approaches to calculating the size of bonuses. This could be a calculation that is tied directly to individuals' investment performance, the revenue from their funds, or a matrix formula of both performance and revenues. There is something to be said for the precision of these calculations, which removes subjectivity and the associated lobbying at year's end. Many employees favor them, as they know where they stand at all points throughout the year. In my observation, however, these types of plans lead to perverse incentives. I have found that large-ego portfolio managers on revenue deals do not play nice in the proverbial sandbox.

I favored a bonus incentive plan that was ultimately discretionary but heavily emphasized investment performance, while leaving something in reserve for a subjective assessment of an individual's nonquantifiable contributions in areas like recruiting, mentorship, and cross-pollinating insights across the other investment teams.

For the quantitative portion, I felt that the experiences of the portfolio manager, analyst, and client should all be aligned. I was a strong believer in measuring everything with precision and ensuring that there were no gaps or residuals in the performance calculation. To this end, every portfolio holding and accompanying benchmark constituent were assigned to a specific analyst. If there was a coverage change, the date of that change was recorded and retained within our performance attribution system. If there was a subsector or industry group that did not have coverage or where portfolio managers were not inclined to invest, then portfolio managers would be assigned those stocks as if they were the analysts. There could be no residual error account; the sum of the performances of the individual analysts would always equal the performance of the portfolio as a whole.

There is much debate within the industry about the time period that should be used for measuring performance. I elected to use a blend of one- and three-year performance, with the three-year figure weighted at 75 percent. There are good arguments for using five years or longer periods, but that introduces issues with how to measure performance for a new joiner, and it also does not align with client expectations since most clients will not tolerate underperformance for more than three years.[3] So, a blend of one year and three years felt like the best compromise.

The final topic under consideration is what form the deferred portion of the bonus should take. For public companies, restricted stock units are often the currency of choice. CEOs and chief financial officers (CFOs) typically like this because it makes employees owners and aligns incentives for everyone at the firm. However, if the firm is large or operates across a diversified set of business lines, the impact of a single employee can be modest, reducing the power of the incentive.

A more enlightened approach is to direct a portion of the bonus into shares in the firm's funds. This is quite common with private equity funds and hedge funds, somewhat less so for mutual fund firms. I liked the concept of our investors "eating their own cooking," so to speak, but I thought that it had the flaw of being dominated by the beta portion of the fund's performance, so I decided to take the idea a step further and isolate the excess return. With the support of our CEO and HR compensation director, I designed a plan that we dubbed "Deferred Alpha" (figure 22.1). Each individual award had a stated initial value that could rise or fall to be

Initial Award Value		**$50,000**
Annualized Excess Return During 3-Year Vesting Period	**Multiplier**	**Final Cash Award**
500+ basis points	**5x**	**$250,000**
300 basis points	**3x**	**$150,000**
100 basis points	**1x**	**$50,000**
0 basis points	**0x**	**$0**
–100 basis points	**0x**	**$0**
–300 basis points	**0x**	**$0**

FIGURE 22.1 Deferred Alpha incentive plan.

worth between zero and five times after three years. The multiplier was a function of the number of percentage points of outperformance. For example, if the fund outperformed by 3 percent per year, the multiplier was 3x. If the fund outperformed by 1 percent per year, the multiplier was 1x, and if the fund either performed in line with its benchmark or trailed it, then the multiplier was zero and there would be no payment. We capped the payout at a multiple of 5x for 5 percent (or greater) annualized outperformance to avoid the perverse incentive of a portfolio manager taking excessive risk. I believe that this incentive plan is unique in the asset management industry and does an excellent job of aligning incentives with the client's experience.

In the Babson College Fund investing class, we face a challenge of misaligned time horizons. Like most college endowments, the fund itself has a goal of achieving attractive risk-adjusted returns over the long term, while the students are motivated to perform well in the current semester. The primary incentive tool is the class grade for each student. The lead professor and the executives-in-residence have debated the optimal grading rubric. I have come to believe that the best approach is to deemphasize short-term investment performance in determining the grade. In its place, I think that tying the grade to the inputs over the outputs makes better sense. Things like level of effort, original thinking, and idea generation are the ingredients of long-term investment success, and these, though subjective, can be assessed over shorter time periods. I believe it is important to reward the process, not just the results.

SOLUTION SUMMARY

1. **Measure what you want managed.** Be precise to avoid having subordinates "manage to the test" rather than pursuing the intended outcome.
2. **Avoid overlooking nonfinancial incentives.** Individuals often value recognition, increased responsibility, and a sense of purpose more than they do extra dollars and cents.
3. **Incentivize inputs over outputs.** Particularly in situations where the outcome will not be known for a long time, or where a heavy element of luck is involved, incentivizing the underlying ingredients to success is key.

Chapter Twenty Three

SELL DISCIPLINE

My favorite holding period is forever.

—Warren Buffett, board chair of Berkshire Hathaway

You know it's time to sell when the shoeshine boy gives you stock tips.

—Joe Kennedy, father of President John F. Kennedy

THE SEVEN SUMMITS. The first time that I saw this phrase was when I was staring at a résumé of an interview candidate at Goldman Sachs. He had taken time off from college to attempt to become the youngest person to climb the highest mountain peak on each of the world's seven continents.

"So, you have climbed Mt. Everest?"

"Yes," he replied.

I recall the hiring manager saying, "While all the other kids were down at the bar, he was training to climb mountains. This guy thinks differently." He got the job.

I was assigned to be his mentor, and we had many lengthy conversations about how to make good risk-adjusted investment decisions, as well as how to manage risk on mountains. One thing that was clear is that the forces of nature, along with basic uncertainty, mean that the best you can hope for is risk *reduction*, not risk *elimination*. My mentee gave me the book *No Shortcuts to the Top*, Ed Viesturs's personal account of his pursuit of climbing the fourteen peaks in the world that were 8,000 meters or higher.[1] In the book, I was struck by how many of the expert climbers whom Viesturs mentioned eventually met an untimely death on a mountain.

These deaths sometimes occurred when the climbers got "summit fever" and exhausted themselves on the ascent, leaving themselves insufficient time or energy to safely complete the descent. "Getting to the top is optional. Getting down is mandatory," as Viesturs says.[2]

Investment decisions are usually not life or death, but the same principle of having an exit plan applies. I am often asked for stock tips, and I am always reluctant to give them. There are several reasons for this, but the main one is that I know that the buy recommendation is only half the equation.

Perhaps the most often-asked question by investment consultants is "What is your sell discipline?" It is an important question because most investors tend to cut their winners and let their losers run.[3]

Most managers give a version of the following answer: "There are three triggers to sell an existing position: (1) It hits our price target, (2) the thesis is disproved, or (3) we find a better opportunity.

There is nothing wrong with any of those three answers. From the manager's point of view, they all are sensible and have the advantage of allowing the portfolio manager to maintain discretion over the decision.

Other portfolio managers (and certain consultants) prefer a rules-based trigger. This could be a fundamental trigger, such as missing a quarterly earnings estimate, a dividend cut, or the departure of an important company executive.[4] It could be a risk-based trigger, such as a cap on position size or contribution to tracking error.[5] Or it could be some sort of technical trading rule based on moving averages or key support levels, although these are not commonplace among professional investors.

An alternative rules-based approach for sell discipline is to use a quantitative trigger such as a stop-loss order. The manager might set this at 10 percent or another value. The benefit of a stop-loss is that it removes emotion, as well as any potential cognitive biases, from the decision. It is simple to understand and straightforward to implement. It also has some basis in the logic that momentum has proved to be a persistent quant factor in markets, so stocks that fall will tend to continue falling.

I know of a portfolio management team that implemented a 15 percent stop-loss sell trigger as part of their process, in part to appeal to investment consultants. During the global financial crisis, the S&P 500 fell 57 percent from peak to trough. This created a problem for the team using the stop loss because the sell-off was so broad based that it would have required them to essentially liquidate their entire portfolio and buy a different set of stocks. They adjusted their rule on the fly so it became a *relative* loss of 15 percent, although even that was hazy because they were not clear with themselves whether they meant relative to the sector or relative to the broad benchmark.

As a value investor, I have never liked stop-loss rules. They go against the contrarian spirit of welcoming the emergence of bargains as stock prices fall.

One value investor who did use a self-imposed rule was Benjamin Graham, Warren Buffett's professor and mentor at Columbia University. He advised:[6]

> The investor should have a definite selling policy for all his common stock commitments, corresponding to his buying techniques. Typically, he should set a reasonable profit objective on each purchase—say 50 to 100 per cent—and a maximum holding period for this objective to be realized—say, two to three years. Purchases not realizing the gain objective at the end of the holding period should be sold out at the market.

Graham reasoned that if an investment had not worked out after two to three years, it was possible that the investor was wrong in the analysis. This is a useful mental frame for avoiding so-called value traps.

Lying between a rigid stop-loss or time-based trigger and a completely subjective approach is one in which a thesis is clearly articulated, and various metrics and their thresholds are documented so a sell decision can be made with quantitative data.[7]

At Eaton Vance, we developed a report that we dubbed "Leaders and Laggards." This was a list of the top and bottom 10 performers in our portfolio over the trailing three-, six-, and twelve-month periods. The report was run weekly and was included in our deck of materials for our internal investment discussions. Any new entrant to the list was marked with an asterisk. We made a point of reviewing the list regularly, with an open mind as to the right course of prospective action.

Another technique was to assign a member of the investment team to be a "Designated Bear" for a specific sector. It was the Bear's duty to poke holes in the thesis and regularly make the case for selling stocks in that secondary coverage area. By constantly probing, we were testing for weak points in the portfolio.

As mentioned in the introduction, the third-party research firm Cabot Research, a subsidiary of FactSet, analyzed every decision on one of our funds over a three-year period and concluded that the largest source of outperformance came from knowing when to sell. I believe that this result was due to the collective impact of the ideas outlined in this book. Having a culture of professional disagreement, where we constantly probed the existing holdings and made it OK to change our minds, supplemented with various portfolio exercises and reports like "Leaders & Laggards," led to a detached perspective where decisions could be made fresh, without the baggage of cognitive bias.

SOLUTION SUMMARY

1. **Set limits.** At the onset of a decision, precommit to a course of action if things go wrong—or right. The limit could be a price or time threshold that you will not allow yourself to breech.
2. **Review leaders as well as laggards.** It is all too easy to focus on problems and leave success to take care of itself. In markets, strong price action can sow the seeds of future failure if prices run ahead of fundamental values.
3. **Designate a bear.** Assign the role of making the sell case for a holding to a member of the team. Instill a culture of dissent throughout the team and reinforce it with incentives.

FINAL REFLECTIONS

WE EACH view the world through our own individual prisms. These prisms are built through the stories that we tell ourselves. They make us uniquely human.

Therein lies the paradox: That which makes us human also makes us fallible. The same mental shortcuts that once kept us alive—and still have a role to play—now undermine our better judgment.

A realistic goal is not to eliminate our biases but to manage them. We can do this with systems, processes, and tools designed to offset our shortcomings—checklists, dissenting voices, natural circuit breakers, and the humility to acknowledge when we get it wrong.

Good judgment is not the absence of mistakes; it's the willingness to confront them.

So, three final thoughts:

Dare to disagree.
Let's embrace uncertainty.
Always look forward.

REFERENCE GUIDE

SUMMARY OF SOLUTIONS

THROUGHOUT THIS book, various tools, tricks, and exercises have been offered as solutions to the biases and challenges that we all share.

These challenges do not exist independent of one another. Certain biases are close cousins or compound one another. For example, overconfidence can amplify the negative impact of any other bias. The good news is that just as the biases overlap, so do the solutions.

These tools are flexible. They can be modified to fit different situations. It is important to understand the goal of each one, but it is not necessary to be dogmatic about its precise application.

Table R.1 is meant to be a quick reference "cheat sheet" of the three solutions provided in the summary of each chapter. Following the table is a longer-form description of the concepts and rationale behind each idea. The concepts have been sorted alphabetically.

TABLE R.1 Quick reference guide to solutions

Bias/Topic	Solution
Action bias	Keep a decision journal.
	Debrief the mission.
	Take advantage of natural circuit breakers.
Analysis paralysis	Split the difference with small positions.
	Practice making low-stakes decisions.
	Simplify.
Anchoring	Use the full toolbox.
	Appoint a devil's advocate.
	Embrace uncertainty.
Building the team	Be decisive during the honeymoon.
	Don't compare notes.
	Use tests for hiring.
Confirmation bias	Ask open-ended questions.
	Phrase questions neutrally.
	Use the 2-4-6 test.
Endowment effect	Perform a zero-based rebuild.
	Find a quitting coach.
	Respect the market.
Framing effect	Use checklists.
	Get a second opinion from a third party.
	Be wary of clichés and axioms.
Grappling with groupthink	Instill a culture of dissent.
	Give subordinates the cover of anonymity.
	The leader speaks last.
Hindsight bias	Write it down.
	Don't believe your lyin' eyes.
	Conduct a postmortem.

Bias/Topic	Solution
Ideal team size	Go for Goldilocks group size. Meetings are invitation only. Engage introverts one-on-one.
Incentives	Measure what you want managed. Avoid overlooking nonfinancial incentives. Incentivize inputs over outputs.
Mental accounting	Reframe your mental accounts. Avoid labels. If you can't beat 'em, join 'em.
Mental models	Go a mile wide and a few inches deep. Avoid over-relying on a single model. Use a latticework of mental models.
Optimism bias	Beware the base rate. Conduct red-team/blue-team drills. Prebrief with premortems.
Outcome bias	Test out of sample. Reward the process. Get the best of it.
Overconfidence	Practice predictions. Make a public confession. Prompt AI to be your biggest critic.
Recency bias	Be a time traveler. Test against your priors. Make use of the multiverse.
Sell discipline	Set limits. Review leaders as well as laggards. Designate a bear.

(*continued*)

TABLE R.1 *(continued)*

Bias/Topic	Solution
Short-termism	Use a discount rate to price the future.
	Act like Robinson Crusoe.
	Set a deadline.
Sunk-cost fallacy	Let it go.
	Always look forward.
	Get a fresh perspective.
Survivorship bias	Reason forward, not backward.
	Identify the full universe.
	Study the losers.
Team culture	Lead by example.
	Use repetition and visual cues.
	Reinforce culture through incentives.
Team versus individual	Identify the decision type.
	Use polls when data is dispersed.
	Experts are best for technical tasks.

ACTION BIAS

Keep a decision journal. The decision journal provides a low-cost method of developing the skill of making decisions when facing uncertainty. It is low cost because no money is being put at risk and no one else ever needs to read the journal. If the decisions are good, confidence will grow. If they are poor, lessons can be learned and course corrections made. A decision journal is a form of practice and feedback, something that athletes engage in regularly but business professionals often neglect.

Debrief the mission. Part of becoming a better decision maker is studying your own track record. Learn from your mistakes as well as your successes. Focus on the process rather than the outcome. What could have been done better? What can be changed going forward? Do this at the end of each project, regardless of outcome.

Take advantage of natural circuit breakers. Many systems and processes have intentional or unintentional circuit breakers to slow things down or offer off-ramps when things start to go wrong. If you suffer from being impetuous, reframe these impediments as tools that you can use to avoid a rushed decision.

ANALYSIS PARALYSIS

Split the difference with small positions. A starter position is a new position in an investment portfolio that has been initiated at less than full weight. When frictional costs are low, apply the concept of starter positions to get past the inertia of analysis paralysis and set things in motion. But be prepared to reverse these decisions quickly if further analysis or information warrants it. Also, do not allow starter positions to accumulate or fester. Splitting the difference is not intended to give permission to "decide not to decide."

Practice making low-stakes decisions. Like most skills, decision making improves with practice. Look for opportunities to make small decisions. When someone else is the decision maker, ask yourself, "What would I have done in that situation?" Force yourself to take a stand and record your decisions in a journal or file, and then review them regularly.

Simplify. Uncertainty can be overwhelming. More data can lead to inaction rather than insight. Try eliminating unlikely options and winnowing down the question or problem to its essence.

ANCHORING

Use the full toolbox. Whether valuing an investment or tackling a different type of complex problem, consider all the tools or mental models that are available and select the best one—or a combination of them—to fit the situation. Resist using the same familiar approach in all situations.

Appoint a devil's advocate. We see the concept of the devil's advocate at work across domains. In the US legal system, we have an adversarial structure, with lawyers making opposing arguments. Presidents sometimes include one or more members of the opposing party in their cabinets or among their advisors. Even inanimate objects can serve this purpose, such as when we lift weights—which provide an opposing force—at the gym. Struggling against an adversary makes us stronger.

Your devil's advocates must sincerely believe their arguments. Otherwise, you risk simply going through the motions of play-acting disagreement rather than working through real conflicts. It is also best if the devil's advocate works independently to avoid anchoring and common-source bias.

Embrace uncertainty. If you are anxious, endeavor to reframe your mind to accept the uncertainty of the future. Embrace the opportunities and excitement that result from not knowing. Take comfort in the fact that others do not know either. Life would be dull if we knew how things will turn out all the time.

BUILDING THE TEAM

Be decisive during the honeymoon. US presidents typically use the first 100 days in office to implement a bold agenda. They recognize that they are fresh off electoral victory, with high public support and a mandate for action. Leaders in other settings can use this same concept by moving quickly to enact any changes that they wish to make.

Don't compare notes. Whenever a subjective assessment is being made by multiple individuals, resist the urge to share opinions before they have been fully formed and written down. It is natural to be curious to see if your assessment is like that of others, but it's better to jot down your conclusions before sharing them to avoid the temptation to conform to the group's consensus. The "wisdom of crowds" works only if the members' inputs are independent.

Use tests for hiring. An objective test of a job applicant's skills reduces the risk that someone is hired simply because they are a skilled interviewee. A test also helps mitigate affinity bias and helps ensure cognitive diversity.

CONFIRMATION BIAS

Ask open-ended questions. We don't know what we don't know, so keep your mind curious and ask questions without presuming the answers. Yes/no questions, as well as "leading the witness" questions, can close off further lines of inquiry and insight.

Phrase questions neutrally. If people are incentivized to tell you what you want to hear, either because they are a subordinate (the "yes man" effect) or because they are attempting to persuade you (the "salesperson" effect), then it is incumbent on you to hide your preconceptions. Phrasing questions in a neutral way is more likely to elicit unbiased information.

Use the 2-4-6 test. Peter Wason's simple test for confirmation bias can reveal the subject's level of curiosity, humility, and reasoning ability, each of which is an important trait for most jobs. Job interview tests can be more objective and revealing than oral conversation and subjective assessment.

THE ENDOWMENT EFFECT

Perform a zero-based rebuild. Whether building an investment portfolio or a budget, start from scratch, with a blank sheet of paper. It is important that the starting point is literally blank. Do not take the status quo and tweak it. Each line item must be justified anew so you avoid falling victim to the inertia and baseline of what is already in place.

Find a quitting coach. Former professional poker player and current decision expert Annie Duke advises having a quitting coach, a specific kind of devil's advocate who can encourage you to throw in the proverbial towel when things are not going well. This could be a trusted friend who advises you on your personal relationships, or it might be a colleague who argues that you should abandon a money-losing project.

Respect the market. The holy grail of investing is to develop what Michael Steinhardt called a "variant perception" on a stock or other investment. However, if the market sustains its disagreement with you over time, it might be you—rather than the market—who is wrong.

THE FRAMING EFFECT

Use checklists. For technical tasks such as piloting an aircraft or performing surgery, checklists are an important tool. The checklist acts as a second set of eyes to ensure that no mundane but important step in the process is overlooked. Checklists can be applied to any repetitive process where the cost of error or omission is high. They are useful when you do not have a partner or colleague to check your work.

Get a second opinion from a third party. Just as with medical advice, it is often a good idea to get the opinion of more than one expert. Importantly, you should find this expert on your own. An opinion from an expert who has been referred to you by the first expert or another interested party is not truly independent. Also, do not share the opinion of the first expert with the second one or you will introduce the risk of anchoring bias.

Be wary of clichés and axioms. Pithy sayings, words that rhyme, catchy tunes . . . these all have the air of authority and accuracy. While memorable and often useful, they are not always reliable. Avoid oversimplifying problems and look for nuance in their complexity.

GRAPPLING WITH GROUPTHINK

Instill a culture of dissent. As the leader of a team or organization, you should want people to actively disagree with one another and to feel totally comfortable airing these differences. You should feel disappointed if you reach an easy consensus. This culture needs to be nurtured and maintained through incentives, or else it will be easy to slip back into the comfort zone of going along to get along.

Give subordinates the cover of anonymity. In large-group settings, subordinates may self-censor. This can be due to shyness, lack of confidence, desire to conform, or respect for the hierarchy of the group. As a leader wishing to hear all perspectives, you need to be creative in eliciting all opinions. Giving anonymity is a great way to do this. For example, conduct a blind vote on important questions. For controversial or uncertain topics, ask that questions be sent ahead of time and shared without attribution.

The leader speaks last. It is important for you, as a leader who values independent perspectives from subordinates, not to reveal a preference. Once your preferences are known, conformity may follow. Let the junior person speak first, as superiors will not feel as constrained by what has already been said.

You speaking first should be reserved for cases where you wish to lead by example, such as publicly confessing to a mistake.

HINDSIGHT BIAS

Write it down. Writing things down brings a measure of accountability. Documenting your opinions at a particular point in time helps guard against a variety of biases, including overconfidence. There is something powerful about reading an erroneous prediction from the past—especially if it is in your own handwriting.

Don't believe your lyin' eyes. Maintain a healthy skepticism about how data is presented. Is anything about it distorted? Is anything being left out? Is a visual story being told by someone with an agenda? Seek out the raw data for yourself.

Conduct a postmortem. Postmortems are a good way to learn from your mistakes. But they are often not used when reviewing successes. If an idea, project, or new product was successful, are you sure that you know why? Were you right for the right reasons, or did you just get lucky? Did something unexpected happen that bailed out an otherwise bad decision? If you wrote out a plan, thesis, or budget with sufficient specificity, then you can test reality versus your forecast.

IDEAL TEAM SIZE

Go for Goldilocks group size. Studies show that for many tasks, a group of three to five individuals is most effective. This number balances the benefits of having a few different perspectives and the constructive debate that follows against the risk of conformity and correlation of errors.

Meetings are invitation only. The larger the audience, the more the individual feels compelled to put on a show. If the group size is too large, controversial perspectives or wild ideas may be muffled. For formal meetings, limit the number of attendees to those who are needed for the discussion.

Engage introverts one-on-one. Individuals vary in their comfort level when speaking in front of peers. You should not assume that someone who elects not to speak has nothing to say. To ensure that valuable insights are not missed, group discussions should be supplemented with private, individual conversations.

INCENTIVES

Measure what you want managed. Be precise when developing incentive structures. Be wary of unintended consequences that can result.

Avoid overlooking nonfinancial incentives. Recognition and a sense of purpose or fulfillment are often more powerful incentives than money. Look for ways to tie these nonfinancial incentives to the organization's goals.

Incentivize inputs over outputs. Individuals often have more control over things like effort, process, and focus than results. Outputs can be influenced by variances caused by external or noncontrollable factors. Tying incentives to inputs creates a fairer reward system and helps to avoid the unwanted effect of "managing to the test."

MENTAL ACCOUNTING

Reframe your mental accounts. To counter the distortions of mental accounting, reaggregate all the "buckets" into a single financial statement. Use the classical economic principles of marginal cost and marginal utility to consider the next and best use of the incremental dollar, regardless of what label you may have previously attached to it. For example, use money from the "rainy day fund" to pay down high-cost revolving debt from a credit card.

Avoid labels. Counter the bias of mental accounting and the poor financial decisions that result from it by avoiding labels for different accounts. Money is money.

If you can't beat 'em, join 'em. Turn the bias of mental accounting on its head to enforce financial self-discipline, such as through automatic payroll deductions to fund retirement accounts.

MENTAL MODELS

Go a mile wide and a few inches deep. Spend time understanding the key contributions from various disciplines in science, sports, philosophy, religion, and literature.

Avoid over-relying on a single model. Eliminate the blind spots that come with overreliance on a single approach. A wide range of perspectives and approaches can yield important insights.

Use a latticework of mental models. Deploy mental models in conjunction with one another. When they suggest different approaches or disagree with one another, put in the effort to understand why rather than taking a simple average or splitting the difference. Celebrate the insights and shortcomings of each model.

OPTIMISM BIAS

Beware the base rate. When making a forecast or evaluating the odds of success, be sure to first study the results of similar examples from the past. At minimum, it will force you to answer the questions, "What do I need to do differently to avoid the high failure rates of others in my endeavor? Why will I be different from the broad averages?"

Conduct red-team/blue-team drills. These simulations started during the 1960s for the purpose of military preparation during the Cold War. They are specific forms of devil's advocacy that are useful in a variety of settings. For example, National Football League (NFL) teams will use scout teams to replicate the opponent's expected style as they practice for an upcoming game. More recently, red-team/blue-team drills have been used by cybersecurity professionals. The red team is charged with attacking a firm's technology systems, and the blue team is tasked with defending them.

Prebrief with premortems. Premortems are a version of the time traveler exercise. When you are facing an uncertain endeavor, search for pitfalls by imagining that you are in the future and failure has already occurred. Write a description of what went wrong (or at least what you think might have gone wrong). This exercise forces you to confront the possibility of failure before the onset of a project, when excitement and confidence are high. It is often less expensive to mitigate risks ahead of time. This exercise can be conducted by a devil's advocate to maximize its effectiveness.

OUTCOME BIAS

Test out of sample. When you have built a prediction model using historical data, test the effectiveness of the model on data that was not used in the construction of the model itself. This statistical best practice can be used even if the model is a simple mental heuristic rather than an elaborate mathematical computer program or spreadsheet.

Reward the process. Acknowledge the presence of variance on outcomes by evaluating—and rewarding—the quality of the decision-making process rather than the outcome. In the long run, this will create a more robust, repeatable form of success.

Get the best of it. As in poker, your goal should be to make the best decisions that you can with the knowledge and information that you have at the time. If you do that, you will always be "getting the best of it," even when statistical variance—dumb luck—undermines an otherwise good decision.

OVERCONFIDENCE

Practice predictions. Fine-tune your confidence level by assigning probabilities to forecasts. Review the accuracy of your calls and determine whether you tend to be overconfident or underconfident when evaluating an uncertain future.

Make a public confession. One of the best ways for you to establish trust as a leader is to admit your mistakes—and to do so publicly. By saying some form of "I got this one wrong. Here's why, and this is what I learned," you will be promoting a culture of learning and sensible risk taking. Periodically encouraging team members to confess mistakes also helps rein in excessive confidence.

This is one case where you, as the leader, should go first. Also, avoid the temptation to sugarcoat or engage in disguised self-flattery—"I am too much of a workaholic" does not count!

Prompt AI to be your biggest critic. Take advantage of emerging technologies like artificial intelligence (AI) chatbots to pressure-test your assumptions and forecasts. Instruct the chat bot to give you its most persuasive critical assessment of your opinion. Unlike humans who may err on the side of diplomacy, your AI tool will pull no punches if prompted properly.

RECENCY BIAS

Be a time traveler. To see things from a different perspective, imagine that you have access to a time machine and you will be writing the headline in the newspaper one year hence. This mental trick allows you to deemphasize the crisis of the moment and take a longer-term perspective. It is also helpful in considering a wider range of potential outcomes than is currently being contemplated.

Test against your priors. To avoid overemphasizing the most recent information, evaluate it in the context of your prior assumptions. If the priors and new information are in conflict, attempt to gather more data and work hard to understand if the new information is simply noise or potentially invalidates your prior understanding. This is a time to use Daniel Kahneman's system 2 mode of thinking.

Make use of the multiverse. The multiverse is the idea that there are multiple universes and small butterfly effects compound into different outcomes across each universe. Like a decision tree, the various nodes splinter. By embracing the uncertainty of the unknown future, you can begin to contemplate different outcomes, assign probabilities, and strike a balance between risk and reward.

SELL DISCIPLINE

Set limits. Limits can take the form of price limits, time limits, or other thresholds. By committing to a course of action at the onset, when emotions are running low, you can remove the risk of posthoc rationalization and thesis drift.

Review leaders as well as laggards. We are all told to "learn from our mistakes." Don't stop there. Study the winners as well as the losers. If you were right, was it for the right reason? It is important not to repeat bad processes that happened to work out this once. Likewise, it might be time to part ways with investments even if they have performed well.

Designate a bear. Designate someone on your team to make the bear case against an idea. This designated individual should take it upon themselves to build sufficient expertise in the subject area such that they can stand toe-to-toe against the proponent of an idea and ensure that it is fully vetted.

SHORT-TERMISM

Use a discount rate to price the future. The concept of a discount rate can be a helpful tool to avoid short-termism. It makes explicit the trade-off between current and future costs and benefits.

Act like Robinson Crusoe. In Daniel Defoe's 1719 classic *Robinson Crusoe*, the eponymous castaway is marooned for twenty-eight years, two months, and nineteen days. *Desert Island Discs*, a radio program on the BBC that began in 1942, asked famous guests to select the music albums that they would take with them if stranded on a desert island. We adopted this idea for stocks but used a five-to-seven-year horizon. You can use this concept to reorient your horizon to the long term. Ask yourself what decision you would make if you had time on your side.

Set a deadline. Procrastination is the bane of the long-term project. Easy, short-term tasks are completed, and long-term value is deferred or sacrificed entirely. Setting firm deadlines, and holding yourself and colleagues accountable to them, ensures the right balance between present and future value.

SUNK-COST FALLACY

Let it go. Professional athletes like pro golfer Greg Norman, Major League Baseball (MLB) relief pitcher Trevor Hoffman, and National Hockey League (NHL) goalie Braden Holtby used visualization techniques for letting go of the highs and lows that come with success and failure in an athletic setting. Whether it is a personal journal or a mental trick of some sort, it is important to develop the skill of letting go.

Always look forward. A Goldman Sachs partner, who was also chief investment officer (CIO) of the Value Equity team, was fond of saying, "Always look forward." What a great way to make decisions and live life in general.

Get a fresh perspective. If a project is not going well, pass it to someone new who can tackle it with a fresh perspective. This might lead to abandoning the project altogether or trying a new approach. Staying the course risks becoming dug in, unwilling to let go of any preconceptions, and fixating on the costs and effort already incurred.

SURVIVORSHIP BIAS

Reason forward, not backward. In analyzing a historical event or data, start at the beginning of the story, with what was known at the time. This will help you avoid both survivorship and outcome bias because any conclusions will be based on the full universe of data, with no filtering based on outcome.

Identify the full universe. When evaluating a dataset, ensure that it is comprehensive. If it has passed a screen or overcome an obstacle, it may not be a reliable universe from which to draw conclusions.

Study the losers. It is common practice to study winners looking for traits to adopt or emulate. Studying losers is sometimes done to learn what *not* to do. A secondary benefit of studying losers can be to identify the false positives of success stories. In other words, if the habits and processes of the winners were also followed by the losers, their benefits should be questioned.

TEAM CULTURE

Lead by example. It is difficult to maintain a consistent culture if the leader's own actions violate their words. The message is reinforced when the action is difficult or has a short-term cost.

Use repetition and visual cues. To reinforce a way of doing things, repeat the message constantly. To indicate what is valued, call attention to it visually.

Reinforce culture through incentives. Public recognition, promotions, and other forms of reward send powerful messages to the individual and the organization. Nothing undermines a culture more than rewarding an individual who is known to have values and behaviors in conflict with the organization's mission.

TEAM VERSUS INDIVIDUAL

Identify the decision type. Certain decisions are best handled by an individual rather than a group. Others benefit from multiple perspectives. Does the decision require technical expertise? Does it require bold assertiveness and a willingness to go against the herd? Take a moment to reflect on the type of decision in question and the decision-making unit and process that are likely to yield the best results.

Use polls when data is dispersed. If no single individual has the answer, taking an average of opinions can be effective, such as making an estimate that requires no special expertise. It is important that individuals be independent of one another to avoid the influence of herding and peer pressure.

Experts are best for technical tasks. When specialized expertise is needed, the decision does not benefit from a large group of uninformed opinions. Flying a plane, performing surgery, and repairing an automobile transmission are examples of tasks that require training and expertise. Even the expert is prone to the occasional mistake so using a checklist or having a second expert review the work is important when the stakes are high.

ACKNOWLEDGMENTS

AFTER THE Bay of Pigs fiasco, President John F. Kennedy famously said, "Success has many fathers, but failure is an orphan."

The ideas in this book have many fathers and mothers. Foremost is Eileen Rominger, who gave me my first shot as an equity analyst, an early chance to pull the trigger as a sector portfolio manager, and the battlefield promotion of an overseas leadership assignment that changed my life. I was incredibly fortunate to find a boss and mentor who saw value in my contrarian, conflict-seeking personality.

Numerous other colleagues at Goldman Sachs Asset Management helped shape my development as an investor and leader. David Berdon was my advocate at the crucial point of joining Goldman Sachs. Sean Gallagher was an early supporter and encouraged me countless times along the way. Rob Crystal was codesigner of "The List," which later transmorphed into "Robinson Crusoe Stocks." Sean Butkus was my devil's advocate and invited me to be his. The late Michael Ho was a kindred spirit in the intellectual pursuit of value investing. Kelly Flynn kept me laughing and prevented me from forgetting my deep value roots. Dan Lochner taught me how to teach and opened my eyes to noninvestment pursuits of risk and reward. Chris Dyer embraced my arrival in London, joined me later at Eaton Vance (ultimately succeeding me there), and was an enthusiast for the investment process and portfolio exercises described in this book, refining and developing several of them himself. Countless other New York–, London-, Brazil-, and Asia-based colleagues made my experience at Goldman Sachs one that I will continue to treasure.

Former colleagues at Eaton Vance deserve collective mention for their talent as investors and willingness to try different approaches. Several of them also taught me about tax-sensitive investing. Individually, I want to thank Michael Keogh for giving me suggestions on an early version of the manuscript and for being my informal advisor on thrift demutualizations. Griff Noble deserves special mention for his intellectual curiosity and willingness to debate investment ideas and design new investment processes. Likewise, I always learned something valuable in my conversations with Andy Valk. Turning dry investment ideas into pithy "isms" like "Be a time traveler" was something I learned from David Richman. Tom Faust always struck the right balance between being supportive in the pursuit of innovative ideas like Deferred Alpha but also probing with the precision of an engineer. He also offered encouragement for an early version of the manuscript.

Michael Mauboussin, with whom I have crossed paths in several capacities (student, client, and colleague) over the past twenty-five years, was the inspiration for several of the ideas and topics herein. Ofir Barnea challenged me to complete an early draft of the manuscript that I had set aside. He later gave me a valuable perspective on the book's application outside the investment sphere. Rad Nova, president and CEO of Junior Achievement of Greater Boston, also offered important feedback from outside the investing realm.

Several others proofread early drafts and offered their opinions, and to them I am thankful. Gabe Samrock went above and beyond, delivering targeted, constructive feedback that could come only from a friend with whom I have been debating for more than thirty-five years starting in college.

Bob Perkin, my father, was another individual who pulled no punches after reading the first draft; his ambition and pursuit of excellence have influenced me from an early age. My mother, Janet Perkin, insurance agent and later artist, inspired me by example as I now undertake my second career.

Matilda Leka did not allow my enthusiasm for this project to peter out, even when things were going slow. Her encouragement was invaluable and ensured the book's completion.

Professional reviewers Jaime Lester and Patrick Gregory will see their fingerprints on the final product. I thank them for their suggestions to expand the target audience to include asset allocators and investment consultants by including chapters on mental models, incentives, and sell discipline.

Finally, I want to thank Brian Smith, my editor, for his support, encouragement, and patience in shepherding the book through the publication process.

NOTES

INTRODUCTION

1. Irving L. Janis, *Groupthink: Psychological Studies of Policy Decisions and Fiascoes*, 2nd ed. (Houghton Mifflin, 1982).
2. Jeffrey Ptak, Amy Arnott, Nikhil Chidurala, Michael Manetta, and Sandeep, *Mind the Gap US 2025*. Morningstar, 2025. Accessed October 15, 2025. https://www.morningstar.com/business/insights/research/mind-the-gap.
3. Source: Morningstar. Performance is gross of expenses and is mentioned for illustrative purposes only. Past performance may not be indicative of future results. The three-year period at GSAM was selected to capture the emerging markets strategies that came under my remit in the latter part of my tenure. The ten-year record at Eaton Vance was selected to approximate my nine-year tenure at the firm.
4. Amos Tversky and Daniel Kahneman, "Prospect Theory: An Analysis of Decision Under Risk," *Econometrica* 47, no. 2 (March 1979): 263–91.
5. Terry Heick, "The Cognitive Biases List: A Visual of 180+ Heuristics," TeachThought, accessed February 10, 2026, https://www.teachthought.com/critical-thinking-posts/cognitive-biases/.
6. Amos Tversky passed away in 1996. The Nobel Prize in Economics is not awarded posthumously, or else Tversky surely would have won the prize alongside his longtime collaborator, Kahneman.

INTRODUCTION

7. Daniel Kahneman, *Thinking, Fast and Slow* (Farrar, Straus and Giroux, 2011).
8. Seth Klarman and Jason Zweig, "Opportunities for Patient Investors," *Financial Analysts Journal* 66, no. 5 (September/October 2010): 1–11.
9. Eugene Fama, "Efficient Capital Markets: A Review of Theory and Empirical Work," *Journal of Finance* 25 (1970): 383–417.
10. Expert network companies are third-party firms that cater to the asset management industry by arranging calls and meetings with members of their network of industry experts who can opine on topics that affect a company or industry. Examples of these experts include doctors, lawyers, and technology professionals, positions for which narrow, specialized knowledge is required.
11. Note that my use of the word "bias" throughout this book refers to cognitive bias or behavioral bias rather than other applications of the term, such as racial, political, or media bias.

1. THE ENDOWMENT EFFECT

1. Daniel Kahneman, Jack L. Knetsch, and Richard H. Thaler, "Experimental Tests of the Endowment Effect," *Journal of Political Economy* 98, no. 6 (1990): 1325–48; Richard H. Thaler, "Toward a Positive Theory of Consumer Choice," *Journal of Economic Behavior and Organization* 1, no. 1 (1980): 39–60.
2. Amos Tversky and Daniel Kahneman, "Prospect Theory: An Analysis of Decision Under Risk," *Econometrica* 47, no. 2 (March 1979): 263–91.
3. Thaler, "Toward a Positive Theory of Consumer Choice."
4. Annie Duke, *Quit: The Power of Knowing When to Walk Away* (Portfolio/Penguin, 2022).

2. SUNK-COST FALLACY

1. Barry M. Staw, "Knee-Deep in the Big Muddy: A Study of Escalating Commitment to a Chosen Course of Action," *Organizational Behavior and Human Performance* 16, no. 1 (1976): 27–44; Richard H. Thaler, "Toward a Positive Theory of Consumer Choice," *Journal of Economic Behavior and Organization* 1, no. 1 (1980): 39–60; Hal R. Arkes and Catherine Blumer, "The Psychology of Sunk Cost," *Organizational Behavior and Human Decision Processes* 35, no. 1 (1985): 124–40.
2. Thaler, "Toward a Positive Theory of Consumer Choice."

3. Traditionally, the term "axe" is used to refer to an analyst on the sell side. It means to be the go-to person on that stock. The axe knows the company better than anyone else, and a change in their opinion will move the stock price because so many investors follow their recommendations.
4. Laurie J. Cameron, "The Mindful Game of Being a Stanley Cup Winner," *PurposeBlue*, June 8, 2018, https://purposeblue.com/the-mindful-game-of-being-a-stanley-cup-winner/, accessed October 15, 2025.

3. HINDSIGHT BIAS

1. Josh Katz, "Hillary Clinton Has an 85 percent Chance to Win," *New York Times*, November 8, 2016.
2. Sam Wang, "Final Projections 2016." *Princeton Election Consortium*, November 8, 2016. https://election.princeton.edu/articles/final-projections-2016/.
3. Nate Silver, "Final Election Update: There's a Wide Range of Outcomes, and Most of Them Come Up Clinton," *FiveThirtyEight*, November 8, 2016, https://fivethirtyeight.com/features/final-election-update-theres-a-wide-range-of-outcomes-and-most-of-them-come-up-clinton/. I think Silver has received insufficient credit for calculating and publishing a number as high as he did. In my opinion, it is wrong to lump him in under the broad criticism, "No one predicted a Trump victory." Under this reasoning, one would have had to give Trump a chance greater than 50 percent to be given credit for prescience. Good prediction models contemplate a range of potential outcomes.
4. Philip Bump, "Donald Trump Will Be President Thanks to 80,000 People in Three States," *Washington Post*, December 1, 2016.
5. Baruch Fischhoff, "Hindsight ≠ Foresight: The Effect of Outcome Knowledge on Judgment Under Uncertainty," *Journal of Experimental Psychology: Human Perception and Performance* 1, no. 3 (1975): 288–99; Jay J. Christensen-Szalanski and Baruch Fischhoff, "Judgment and Decision Making: Human Performance in Decision Making," *Organizational Behavior and Human Performance* 33, no. 1 (1984): 1–29.
6. Fischhoff, "Hindsight ≠ Foresight."

4. OUTCOME BIAS

1. Jonathan Baron and John C. Hershey, "Outcome Bias in Decision Evaluation," *Journal of Personality and Social Psychology* 54, no. 4 (1988): 569–79.

2. Brian Burke, "Expected Points," *Advanced Football Analytics*, August 2008, http://www.advancedfootballanalytics.com/2008/08/expected-points.html.

   "Expected points" is a concept that has been developed by quantitative sports analysts to capture the full picture of a player or team's situation, decision, or performance. In the case of a team on its own ten-yard line (or less), the team on defense is more likely to score before the team on offense. In other words, field position is so poor that the team with the ball is worse off for having possession.
3. One nuance to this analysis is that it does not solely depend on the score differential; it also depends on the time remaining in the game. When making any type of decision early in the game of any sport, a team should be primarily focused on maximizing expected points. As the game moves toward its conclusion, a team should make decisions that maximize its probability of winning, a somewhat different concept. In general, the leading team should act more conservatively, and the trailing team should increasingly take risks, to the point of doing things that would have been reckless earlier in the game. Other variations of this variance-seeking concept include Hail Mary attempts, onside kicks, pulling the goalie in hockey, and committing intentional fouls in basketball.
4. For unconventional strategies, I had in mind scenarios such as intentionally allowing the opponent to score to regain possession of the ball, a decision that Mike Holmgren, head coach of the Green Bay Packers, made in Super Bowl XXXII.
5. Michael Wilbon, *Pardon the Interruption.* ESPN, January 22, 2024.
6. I use the term "dumb luck" to describe variance or statistical chance, not in the superstitious sense.
7. Baron and Hershey, "Outcome Bias in Decision Evaluation."
8. "The Superinvestors of Graham-and-Doddsville," *Wikipedia: The Free Encyclopedia.* https://en.wikipedia.org/wiki/The_Superinvestors_of_Graham-and-Doddsville, last edited October 4, 2025; accessed January 21, 2026.
9. Warren E. Buffett, "The Superinvestors of Graham-and-Doddsville," *Hermes: Columbia Business School Magazine* (Fall 1984), https://www8.gsb.columbia.edu/articles/hermes/superinvestors.
10. For simplicity in this example, I am ignoring advanced concepts like "implied odds," where further betting is possible after the river card. I am also ignoring the option of reraising as a bluff.

11. Showing undealt cards is bad form and against the spirit of the game, as it potentially reveals information about the opponent's unseen hand, to which the player is not entitled without calling the bet.

5. SURVIVORSHIP BIAS

1. "Abraham Wald: A Statistical Hero," *History of Data Science*, June 3, 2021, https://www.historyofdatascience.com/abraham-wald-a-statistical-hero/.
2. Stephen J. Brown, William N. Goetzmann, and Roger G. Ibbotson, "Survivorship Bias in Performance Studies," *Review of Financial Studies* 5, no. 4 (1992): 553–80.
3. *Tracking error* is a measure of how much the performance of an investment portfolio differs from that of another portfolio or index.
4. Ian Webster, "Stock Market Returns Since 1900," *Official Data Foundation*, data sourced from Robert Shiller, Irrational Exuberance (Princeton University Press), http://www.officialdata.org/us/stocks/s-p-500/1900.
5. Anthony Randazzo and Jonathan Moody, "State of Pensions 2025," Equable Institute. https://equable.org/state-of-pensions-2025/.
6. James Eagle, "Animation: Stock Market vs. GDP Share, by Country (1900–2022)," *Visual Capitalist*, https://www.visualcapitalist.com/cp/stock-market-and-gdp-shares/.
7. Elroy Dimson, Paul Marsh, and Mike Staunton, *Credit Suisse Global Investment Returns Yearbook 2020* (Credit Suisse Research Institute, 2020).

6. THE FRAMING EFFECT

1. Amos Tversky and Daniel Kahneman, "The Framing of Decisions and the Psychology of Choice," *Science* 211, no. 4481 (January 30, 1981): 453–58.
2. Barbara J. McNeil, Stephen G. Paucker, Harold C. Sox Jr., and Amos Tversky, "On the Elicitation of Preferences for Alternative Therapies," *New England Journal of Medicine* 306, no. 21 (1982): 1259–62.
3. I realize that I am offering a highly controversial viewpoint with which many will disagree. My point is to encourage the reader to think through simple rules of thumb and phrases rather than accept them at face value. This includes when you are the originator of the frame yourself.

6. THE FRAMING EFFECT

4. Benjamin Graham and Jason Zweig, *The Intelligent Investor: The Definitive Book on Value Investing*, 3rd ed. (Harper Business, 2024).

7. MENTAL ACCOUNTING

1. Richard H. Thaler, "Mental Accounting Matters," *Journal of Behavioral Decision Making* 12, no. 3 (September 1999): 183–206.
2. This suggestion assumes that the individual has enough self-control to avoid running up new credit card bills simply because there is available credit.
3. Richard H. Thaler and Cass R. Sunstein, *Nudge: Improving Decisions About Health, Wealth, and Happiness* (Yale University Press, 2008). Despite its influence, *Nudge* has come under criticism for being paternalistic. This nuanced suggestion is for individuals to choose to use the principle of nudging on themselves, making them willing actors.

8. ANCHORING

1. Amos Tversky and Daniel Kahneman, "Judgment Under Uncertainty: Heuristics and Biases," *Science* 185, no. 4157 (September 27, 1974): 1124–31.
2. As discussed in chapter 5, on survivorship bias, this number is probably a bit too high, but it's a round figure that works for this purpose. A lower required rate of return would only make the point more dramatically.

9. RECENCY BIAS

1. Mark Heisler, "Portland Gives, Jordan Takes—Three at a Time," *Los Angeles Times*, June 4, 1992, https://www.latimes.com/archives/la-xpm-1992-06-04-sp-1212-story.html.
2. Thomas Gilovich, Robert Vallone, and Amos Tversky, "The Hot Hand in Basketball: On the Misperception of Random Sequences," *Cognitive Psychology* 17, no. 3 (July 1985): 295–314.
3. Aubrey Clayton, "The Hot Hand Is Not a Myth," *Nautilus*, June 7, 2024. https://nautil.us/the-hot-hand-is-not-a-myth-643539/.
4. Joshua B. Miller and Adam Sanjurjo, "Surprised by the Hot Hand Fallacy? A Truth in the Law of Small Numbers," *Econometrica* 86, no. 6 (December 2018): 2019–47.

5. Gur Yaari and Shmuel Eisenmann, "The Hot (Invisible?) Hand: Can Time Sequence Patterns of Success/Failure in Sports Be Modeled as Repeated Random Independent Trials?" *PLOS One* 6, no. 6 (June 8, 2011), https://doi.org/10.1371/journal.pone.0024532.
6. Hermann Ebbinghaus, *Memory: A Contribution to Experimental Psychology*, trans. Henry A. Ruger and Clara E. Bussenius (Teachers College, Columbia University, 1913), originally published in 1885.
7. Henry Glanzer and Anita R. Cunitz, "Two Storage Mechanisms in Free Recall," *Journal of Verbal Learning and Verbal Behavior* 5, no. 4 (1966): 351–60.
8. With increased regulatory scrutiny, this practice is more subtle and less prevalent than in the past. In the late 1990s, corporate investor relations personnel often made phone calls to sell-side analysts with high estimates to explicitly encourage them to lower their numbers. The sell-side analysts were happy to receive this information, as it allowed them to improve the accuracy of their published estimates and pass the information to favored clients.
9. This quote is attributed to Elroy Dimson of the London Business School.

10. SHORT-TERMISM

1. Aesop, *The Fables of Aesop: Selected, Told Anew, and Their History Traced*, translated by Joseph Jacobs (public domain: Project Gutenberg, published November 2, 2023). https://www.gutenberg.org/files/28/28-h/28-h.htm.
2. For the sake of simplicity, I am ignoring the unusual case of negative interest rates and the cost of physically safeguarding money.
3. "Martín de Azpilcueta," *Wikipedia: The Free Encyclopedia*, last modified January 23, 2024, https://en.wikipedia.org/wiki/Mart%C3%ADn_de_Azpilcueta.
4. Cade Massey and Richard H. Thaler, "The Loser's Curse: Decision Making and Market Efficiency in the National Football League Draft," *Management Science* 59, no. 7 (July 2013): 1479–95.
5. Mark Desjardine and Pratima Bansal, "Failure to Meet Analysts' Expectations: How Financial Markets Contribute to Corporate Short-Termism," *SSRN Electronic Journal*, January 1, 2015.

10. SHORT-TERMISM

6. Peter Lynch and John Rothchild, *One Up on Wall Street: How to Use What You Already Know to Make Money in the Market* (Simon & Schuster, 2000). Admittedly, I may be engaging in survivorship bias by selecting this example to illustrate the point.

11. CONFIRMATION BIAS

1. Kassiani Nikolopoulou, "What Is Confirmation Bias? | Definition & Examples," *Scribbr*, September 19, 2022, revised March 10, 2023.
2. "Confirmation Bias," *Wikipedia: The Free Encyclopedia*. https://en.wikipedia.org/wiki/Confirmation_bias.
3. Peter Wason, "On the Failure to Eliminate Hypotheses in a Conceptual Task," *Quarterly Journal of Experimental Psychology* 12, no. 3 (1960): 129–40.
4. Christophe de Margerie died three years later in a mysterious airplane accident on a runway in Moscow.
5. I am not suggesting that material, nonpublic information was sought or received. Management teams can be very guarded even when discussing matters of public record, particularly when the business is underperforming.

12. ANALYSIS PARALYSIS

1. Jeffrey P. Bezos, "2016 Letter to Shareholders," Amazon.com, Inc., April 17, 2017, https://www.aboutamazon.com/news/company-news/2016-letter-to-shareholders.
2. Barry Schwartz, *The Paradox of Choice: Why More Is Less* (HarperCollins, 2004); Sheena S. Iyengar and Mark R. Lepper, "When Choice Is Demotivating: Can One Desire Too Much of a Good Thing?" *Journal of Personality and Social Psychology* 79, no. 6 (2000): 995–1006.
3. Daniel Ellsberg, "Risk, Ambiguity, and the Savage Axioms," *Quarterly Journal of Economics* 75, no. 4 (1961): 643–69.
4. It is worth noting that there can be times when very small positions are appropriate. For example, in the small-cap biotechnology industry, where the price of the common stock of these early-stage, cash-burning, high-potential companies can either go to zero or increase tenfold, a "basket approach," where one owns several stocks, each of a small size, would represent sensible diversification and risk management.

5. Paper journals work best in my opinion, but good electronic versions are also available, including Grid Diary, Joplin, Penzu, Diarium, and Day One.
6. Despite this insight, pitch books reverted to their unnecessary length. Cultural traditions are sticky.
7. Jeff Bezos, "Jeff Bezos: Amazon and Blue Origin | Lex Fridman Podcast #405," YouTube video, December 14, 2023, https://www.youtube.com/watch?v=DcWqzZ3I2cY.
8. In chess, *zugzwang* is a position where every potential move leads to a worse position.

13. ACTION BIAS

1. Michael Bar-Eli, Ofer H. Azar, Ilana Ritov, Yair Keidar-Levin, and Galit Schein, "Action Bias Among Elite Soccer Goalkeepers: The Case of Penalty Kicks," *Journal of Economic Psychology* 28, no. 5 (October 2007): 606–21.
2. InnerDrive Team, "The Sport Psychology of Perfect Penalties," ed. Bradley Busch. InnerDrive. https://www.innerdrive.co.uk/blog/psychology-perfect-penalties/, accessed January 22, 2026.
3. Anthony Patt and Richard Zeckhauser, "Action Bias and Environmental Decisions," *Journal of Risk and Uncertainty* 21 (2000): 45–72.
4. Amity Shlaes, *Coolidge* (New York: Harper, 2013).
5. "C-SPAN Presidential Historians Survey, 2021," C-SPAN. https://www.c-span.org/presidentsurvey2021, accessed October 15, 2025.
6. "Analysis Paralysis," *Wikipedia: The Free Encyclopedia*, https://en.wikipedia.org/wiki/Analysis_paralysis, accessed October 15, 2025.

14. OPTIMISM BIAS

1. The Dunes Hotel and Casino was on the famous "four corners" of the Las Vegas Strip, where the Bellagio Hotel and Casino now sits. These days, one is lucky to find a $25 minimum table played out of a shoe that still pays 3–2 on blackjack and does not use a machine to shuffle after every hand.
2. Neil D. Weinstein, "Unrealistic Optimism About Future Life Events," *Journal of Personality and Social Psychology* 39, no. 5 (November 1980): 806–20.

14. OPTIMISM BIAS

3. Michael Mauboussin is a legendary Wall Street strategist and thinker who worked for many years at Credit Suisse and Legg Mason. I first came across Mauboussin at Columbia Business School, where he teaches an investing course. I was a client of his for many years, and he later became a colleague, as we both worked for affiliated equity teams at Morgan Stanley.

15. OVERCONFIDENCE

1. Ola Svenson, "Are We All Less Risky and More Skillful than Our Fellow Drivers?" *Acta Psychologica* 47, no. 2 (1981): 143–48.
2. Philip E. Tetlock and Dan Gardner, *Superforecasting: The Art and Science of Prediction* (Crown Publishers, 2015).
3. Chase Kennedy, "Age vs. Wear and Tear: The Deterioration of an NFL Running Back." Undergraduate thesis, Haverford College, 2010.

16. GRAPPLING WITH GROUPTHINK

1. Diane Vaughan, *The Challenger Launch Decision: Risky Technology, Culture, and Deviance at NASA* (University of Chicago Press, 1996).
2. Irving L. Janis, *Groupthink: Psychological Studies of Policy Decisions and Fiascoes*, 2nd ed. (Houghton Mifflin, 1982); James K. Esser, "Alive and Well After 25 Years: A Review of Groupthink Research," *Organizational Behavior and Human Decision Processes* 73, no. 2–3 (1998): 116–41.
3. Saul McLeod, "Asch Conformity Line Experiment," *SimplyPsychology*. https://www.simplypsychology.org/asch-conformity.html, updated May 15, 2025.

17. TEAM VERSUS INDIVIDUAL

1. Jan Lorenz, Heiko Rauhut, Frank Schweitzer, and Dirk Helbing, "How Social Influence Can Undermine the Wisdom of Crowd Effect," *Proceedings of the National Academy of Sciences* 108, no. 22 (2011): 9020–25.
2. Charles Mackay, *Extraordinary Popular Delusions and the Madness of Crowds* (Wordsworth Editions, 1995).
3. James Surowiecki, *The Wisdom of Crowds* (Doubleday, 2004).
4. Albert Mannes, Jack Soll, and Richard Larrick, "The Wisdom of Select Crowds," *Journal of Personality and Social Psychology* 107, no. 2 (2014): 276–99.

5. Cliff Asness, post on X (formerly Twitter), September 2, 2023. https://x.com/CliffordAsness/status/1698016836930212097.
6. "Cash drag" is the performance drag of a portfolio when it is compared to a benchmark, such as the S&P 500, that has tended to outperform the investment return on cash over time. For example, if 5 percent of the portfolio is held in cash and the S&P 500 outperforms by 10 percent per year, the performance shortfall will be 0.5 percent (5 percent x 10 percent), or 50 basis points annually. There are various tools that portfolio managers can use to mitigate this performance drag, but many elect not to use them, which is a major source of underperformance across the asset management industry. Incidentally, I believe that Eaton Vance is best-in-class at minimizing the effects of cash drag.

18. IDEAL TEAM SIZE

1. Jaimie Arona Krems and Jason Wilkes, "Why Are Conversations Limited to About Four People? A Theoretical Exploration of the Conversation Size Constraint," *Evolution and Human Behavior* 40, no. 2 (March 2019): 140–47.
2. Robin I. M. Dunbar, "Neocortex Size as a Constraint on Group Size in Primates," *Journal of Human Evolution* 22, no. 6 (1992): 469–93; "Dunbar's Number: Why We Can Only Maintain 150 Relationships," *BBC Future*, October 9, 2019, https://www.bbc.com/future/article/20191001-dunbars-number-why-we-can-only-maintain-150-relationships.
3. Marcia Blenko, Michael Mankins, and Paul Rogers, *Decide & Deliver: 5 Steps to Breakthrough Performance in Your Organization* (Harvard Business Review Publishing, 2010).
4. Jaime Potter, "The Ideal Team Size at Work May Be Smaller Than You Think," *Forbes*, April 27, 2020, https://www.forbes.com/sites/jaimepotter/2020/04/27/the-ideal-team-size-at-work-may-be-smaller-than-you-think/.

19. BUILDING THE TEAM

1. Herminia M. Ibarra and Nicole Sackley, *Charlotte Beers at Ogilvy & Mather Worldwide (A)*, Harvard Business School Case 495-031, January 1995 (revised September 2011).

19. BUILDING THE TEAM

2. Buffett's $5 billion investment took the form of preferred stock, with warrants to purchase a further $5 billion of common stock at the attractive price of $115 per share. The design of this investment was very clever: It gave him an attractive current dividend of 10 percent, a higher position in the capital structure than common stockholders in the event of a liquidation, but it also preserved all the upside of the common stock via the warrants. At the time, I found it odd that the financial media described this as a show of confidence in the firm. Buffett's unique risk/return profile was very different from that of investors who owned the firm's common stock.
3. *The Wolf of Wall Street*, directed by Martin Scorsese (Paramount Pictures, 2013).

20. TEAM CULTURE

1. Margaret Heffernan, "Dare to Disagree," *TEDGlobal 2012*, June 2012, https://www.ted.com/talks/margaret_heffernan_dare_to_disagree.
2. Kim S. Cameron and Robert E. Quinn, *Diagnosing and Changing Organizational Culture: Based on the Competing Values Framework*, 3rd ed. (Wiley, 2011).

21. MENTAL MODELS

1. David Spira, "Solve This Crossword in Less Than 12 Minutes and You Could Have Been a WWII Codebreaker," *Room Escape Artist*, February 11, 2017, https://roomescapeartist.com/2017/02/11/solve-this-crossword-in-less-than-12-minutes-and-you-could-have-been-a-wwii-codebreaker/.
2. "Latticework of mental models" is a term used by Charlie Munger to describe the benefits of drawing insights and expertise from different disciplines. The book *Poor Charlie's Almanack* (Donning, 2005), by Munger, highlights these insights from speeches that he gave to college students. Robert Hagstrom, *Latticework: The New Investing* (Texere, 2000), expands on Munger's ideas.
3. Shane Parrish, "Mental Models: The Best Way to Make Intelligent Decisions (~100 Models Explained)," *Farnam Street*, accessed October 14, 2025, https://fs.blog/mental-models/.

22. INCENTIVES

1. Uri Gneezy and Aldo Rustichini, "Pay Enough or Don't Pay at All," *Quarterly Journal of Economics* 115, no. 3 (2000): 791–810.
2. Steven D. Levitt and Stephen J. Dubner, *Freakonomics: A Rogue Economist Explores the Hidden Side of Everything* (William Morrow, 2005); Richard H. Thaler and Cass R. Sunstein, *Nudge: Improving Decisions About Health, Wealth, and Happiness* (Yale University Press, 2008); Daniel H. Pink, *Drive: The Surprising Truth About What Motivates Us* (Riverhead, 2009).
3. Jeremy Grantham, "GMO Quarterly Letter: My Sister's Pension Assets and Agency Problems (The Tension Between Protecting Your Job or Your Clients' Money)," *GMO*, April 2012, https://www.scribd.com/doc/92773801/GMO-Quarterly-Letter-My-Sister-s-Pension-Assets-0412-GMO-Grantham.

23. SELL DISCIPLINE

1. Ed Viesturs with David Roberts, *No Shortcuts to the Top: Climbing the World's Fourteen Highest Peaks* (Broadway, 2006).
2. Viesturs, *No Shortcuts to the Top*, 11.
3. Hersh Shefrin and Meir Statman, "The Disposition to Sell Winners Too Early and Ride Losers Too Long," *Journal of Finance* 40, no. 3 (1985): 777–90.
4. In one of our "two mistakes I made last year" exercises, a former colleague admonished himself with the words, "No matter what the company tells you, it is always a red flag when a CFO leaves unexpectedly."
5. I prefer risk-based or active-weight-based limits. When managing risk versus using a benchmark, imposing position limits in absolute terms, or as a multiple of the constituent's weight in the benchmark, has the effect of treating the risk contribution of positions differently. Risk management is the main point of sell discipline in the first place.
6. Benjamin Graham and Jason Zweig, *The Intelligent Investor: The Definitive Book on Value Investing*, 3rd ed. (Harper Business, 2024).
7. Michael J. Mauboussin and Dan Callahan, "If You Can't Measure It, You Can't Manage It: Improving the Art and Science of Sell Decisions," *Credit Suisse Global Financial Strategies* (2016).

BIBLIOGRAPHY

"Action Bias." *Wikipedia: The Free Encyclopedia.* https://en.wikipedia.org/wiki/Action_bias. Last modified January 30, 2024; accessed October 15, 2025.

Aesop. *The Fables of Aesop: Selected, Told Anew, and Their History Traced.* Trans. Joseph Jacobs. Project Gutenberg, November 2, 2023. https://www.gutenberg.org/files/28/28-h/28-h.htm, accessed October 15, 2025.

"Analysis Paralysis." *Wikipedia: The Free Encyclopedia.* https://en.wikipedia.org/wiki/Analysis_paralysis. Last modified January 9, 2024; accessed October 15, 2025.

Arkes, Hal R., and Catherine Blumer. "The Psychology of Sunk Cost." *Organizational Behavior and Human Decision Processes* 35, no. 1 (1985): 124–40.

Asness, Cliff. "Post on X (formerly Twitter)." September 2, 2023. https://x.com/CliffordAsness/status/1698016836930212097. Accessed October 15, 2025.

Bar-Eli, Michael, Ofer H. Azar, Ilana Ritov, Yair Keidar-Levin, and Galit Schein. "Action Bias Among Elite Soccer Goalkeepers: The Case of Penalty Kicks." *Journal of Economic Psychology* 28, no. 5 (October 2007): 606–21.

Baron, Jonathan, and John C. Hershey. "Outcome Bias in Decision Evaluation." *Journal of Personality and Social Psychology* 54, no. 4 (1988): 569–79.

BBC Future. "Dunbar's Number: Why We Can Only Maintain 150 Relationships." *BBC Future*, October 9, 2019. https://www.bbc.com/future/article/20191001-dunbars-number-why-we-can-only-maintain-150-relationships. Accessed October 15, 2025.

Bernstein, Peter L. *Against the Gods: The Remarkable Story of Risk.* Wiley, 1996.

Bezos, Jeffrey P. "2016 Letter to Shareholders." Amazon.com, April 17, 2017.

Bezos, Jeffrey P. "Jeff Bezos: Amazon and Blue Origin | Lex Fridman Podcast #405." YouTube video, December 14, 2023. https://www.youtube.com/watch?v=DcWqzZ3I2cY. Accessed October 15, 2025.

Blenko, Marcia W., Michael C. Mankins, and Paul Rogers. *Decide & Deliver: 5 Steps to Breakthrough Performance in Your Organization.* Harvard Business Review Press, 2010.

Brown, Stephen J., William N. Goetzmann, and Roger G. Ibbotson. "Survivorship Bias in Performance Studies." *Review of Financial Studies* 5, no. 4 (1992): 553–80.

Bump, Philip. "Donald Trump Will Be President Thanks to 80,000 People in Three States." *The Washington Post*, December 1, 2016.

Buffett, Warren E. "The Superinvestors of Graham-and-Doddsville." *Hermes: Columbia Business School Magazine* (Fall 1984). https://www8.gsb.columbia.edu/articles/hermes/superinvestors. Accessed October 15, 2025.

Burke, Brian. "Expected Points." *Advanced Football Analytics*, August 2008. http://www.advancedfootballanalytics.com/2008/08/expected-points.html. Accessed October 15, 2025.

Cameron, Kim S., and Robert E. Quinn. *Diagnosing and Changing Organizational Culture: Based on the Competing Values Framework.* 3rd ed. Wiley, 2011.

Cameron, Laurie J. "The Mindful Game of Being a Stanley Cup Winner." *PurposeBlue*, June 8, 2018. https://purposeblue.com/the-mindful-game-of-being-a-stanley-cup-winner/. Accessed October 15, 2025.

Christensen-Szalanski, Jay J., and Baruch Fischhoff. "Judgment and Decision Making: Human Performance in Decision Making." *Organizational Behavior and Human Performance* 33, no. 1 (1984): 1–29.

Cialdini, Robert B. *Influence: The Psychology of Persuasion.* Harper Business, 2006.

Clayton, Aubrey. "The Hot Hand Is Not a Myth." *Nautilus*, June 7, 2024. https://nautil.us/the-hot-hand-is-not-a-myth-643539/. Accessed October 15, 2025.

"Confirmation Bias." *Wikipedia: The Free Encyclopedia.* https://en.wikipedia.org/wiki/Confirmation_bias. Last modified October 2025; accessed October 15, 2025.

Desjardine, Mark, and Pratima Bansal. "Failure to Meet Analysts' Expectations: How Financial Markets Contribute to Corporate Short-Termism." *SSRN Electronic Journal*, October 14, 2015.

Dimson, Elroy, Paul Marsh, and Mike Staunton. *Credit Suisse Global Investment Returns Yearbook 2020*. Credit Suisse Research Institute, 2020.

Dunbar, Robin I. M. "Neocortex Size as a Constraint on Group Size in Primates." *Journal of Human Evolution* 22, no. 6 (1992): 469–93.

Duke, Annie. *How to Decide: Simple Tools for Making Better Choices*. Portfolio /Penguin, 2020.

Duke, Annie. *Quit: The Power of Knowing When to Walk Away*. Portfolio/Penguin, 2022.

Duke, Annie. *Thinking in Bets: Making Smarter Decisions When You Don't Have All the Facts*. Portfolio/Penguin, 2019.

Gawande, Atul. *The Checklist Manifesto: How to Get Things Right*. Metropolitan, 2009.

Eagle, James. "Animation: Stock Market vs. GDP Share, by Country (1900–2022)." *Visual Capitalist*. https://www.visualcapitalist.com/cp/stock-market-and-gdp-shares. Accessed October 15, 2025.

Ebbinghaus, Hermann. *Memory: A Contribution to Experimental Psychology*. Trans. Henry A. Ruger and Clara E. Bussenius. Teachers College, Columbia University, 1913. Originally published in 1885.

Ellsberg, Daniel. "Risk, Ambiguity, and the Savage Axioms." *Quarterly Journal of Economics* 75, no. 4 (1961): 643–69.

Esser, James K. "Alive and Well After 25 Years: A Review of Groupthink Research." *Organizational Behavior and Human Decision Processes* 73, no. 2–3 (1998): 116–41.

Fischhoff, Baruch. "Hindsight ≠ Foresight: The Effect of Outcome Knowledge on Judgment Under Uncertainty." *Journal of Experimental Psychology: Human Perception and Performance* 1, no. 3 (1975): 288–99.

Garland, Howard. "Throwing Good Money After Bad: The Effect of Sunk Costs on the Decision to Continue a Project." *Journal of Applied Psychology* 75, no. 6 (1990): 728–31.

Gilovich, Thomas. *How We Know What Isn't So: The Fallibility of Human Reason in Everyday Life*. Free Press, 1993.

Gilovich, Thomas, Robert Vallone, and Amos Tversky. "The Hot Hand in Basketball: On the Misperception of Random Sequences." *Cognitive Psychology* 17, no. 3 (July 1985): 295–314.

Gladwell, Malcolm. *Blink: The Power of Thinking Without Thinking*. Back Bay, 2007.

Gladwell, Malcolm. *Outliers: The Story of Success*. Back Bay, 2011.

Glanzer, Henry, and Anita R. Cunitz. "Two Storage Mechanisms in Free Recall." *Journal of Verbal Learning and Verbal Behavior* 5, no. 4 (1966): 351–60.

Gneezy, Uri, and Aldo Rustichini. "Pay Enough or Don't Pay at All." *Quarterly Journal of Economics* 115, no. 3 (2000): 791–810.

Graham, Benjamin, and Jason Zweig. *The Intelligent Investor: The Definitive Book on Value Investing.* 3rd ed. Harper Business, 2024.

Grantham, Jeremy. "GMO Quarterly Letter: My Sister's Pension Assets and Agency Problems (The Tension Between Protecting Your Job or Your Clients' Money)." *GMO*, April 2012. https://www.gmo.com/globalassets/articles/quarterly-letter/2012/my-sisters-pension_jeremy-grantham_apr2012.pdf

Hagstrom, Robert G. *Latticework: The New Investing.* Texere, 2000.

Heffernan, Margaret. "Dare to Disagree." *TEDGlobal 2012.* June 2012. https://www.ted.com/talks/margaret_heffernan_dare_to_disagree. Accessed October 15, 2025.

Heick, Terry. "The Cognitive Biases List: A Visual of 180+ Heuristics." *TeachThought.* https://www.teachthought.com/critical-thinking-posts/cognitive-biases/. Accessed February 10, 2026.

Ibarra, Herminia M., and Nicole Sackley. *Charlotte Beers at Ogilvy & Mather Worldwide (A).* Harvard Business School Case 495–031. January 1995; revised September 2011.

InnerDrive Team. "The Sport Psychology of Perfect Penalties." Edited by Bradley Busch. *InnerDrive.* https://www.innerdrive.co.uk/blog/psychology-perfect-penalties/. Accessed October 15, 2025.

Iyengar, Sheena S., and Mark R. Lepper. "When Choice Is Demotivating: Can One Desire Too Much of a Good Thing?" *Journal of Personality and Social Psychology* 79, no. 6 (2000): 995–1006.

Janis, Irving L. *Groupthink: Psychological Studies of Policy Decisions and Fiascoes.* 2nd ed. Houghton Mifflin, 1982.

Jensen, Michael C. "Some Anomalous Evidence Regarding Market Efficiency." *Journal of Financial Economics* 6, nos. 2–3 (June–September 1978): 95–101.

Kahneman, Daniel. *Thinking, Fast and Slow.* Farrar, Straus and Giroux, 2011.

Kahneman, Daniel, Jack L. Knetsch, and Richard H. Thaler. "Experimental Tests of the Endowment Effect and the Coase Theorem." *Journal of Political Economy* 98, no. 6 (December 1990): 1325–48.

Kennedy, Chase. "Age vs. Wear and Tear: The Deterioration of an NFL Running Back." Thesis, Haverford College, 2010.

Klarman, Seth, and Jason Zweig. "Opportunities for Patient Investors." *Financial Analysts Journal* 66, no. 5 (September/October 2010): 1–11.

Klosterman, Chuck. *But What If We're Wrong: Thinking About the Present as If It Were the Past.* Penguin, 2016.

Krems, Jaimie Arona, and Jason Wilkes. "Why Are Conversations Limited to About Four People? A Theoretical Exploration of the Conversation Size Constraint." *Evolution and Human Behavior* 40, no. 2 (March 2019): 140–47.

Leslie, Ian. *Conflicted: How Productive Disagreements Lead to Better Outcomes.* Harper Business, 2021.

Lewis, Michael. *Moneyball: The Art of Winning an Unfair Game.* Norton, 2004.

Lieberman, David J. *Never Be Lied to Again.* St. Martin's Press, 2000.

Lindbergh, Ben, and Sam Miller. *The Only Rule Is It Has to Work: Our Wild Experiment Building a New Kind of Baseball Team.* St. Martin's Griffin, 2017.

Lorenz, Jan, Heiko Rauhut, Frank Schweitzer, and Dirk Helbing. "How Social Influence Can Undermine the Wisdom of Crowd Effect." *Proceedings of the National Academy of Sciences* 108, no. 22 (2011): 9020–25.

Lynch, Peter, and John Rothchild. *One Up on Wall Street: How to Use What You Already Know to Make Money in the Market.* Simon & Schuster, 2000.

Mackay, Charles. *Extraordinary Popular Delusions and the Madness of Crowds.* Wordsworth Editions, 1995.

McLeod, Saul. "Asch Conformity Line Experiment." *SimplyPsychology.* https://www.simplypsychology.org/asch-conformity.html. Updated May 15, 2025; accessed October 15, 2025.

McNeil, Barbara J., Stephen G. Pauker, Harold C. Cox Jr., and Amos Tversky. "On the Elicitation of Preferences for Alternative Therapies." *New England Journal of Medicine* 306, no. 21 (1982): 1259–62.

Mannes, Albert, Jack Soll, and Richard Larrick. "The Wisdom of Select Crowds." *Journal of Personality and Social Psychology* 107, no. 2 (2014): 276–99.

"Martín de Azpilcueta." *Wikipedia: The Free Encyclopedia.* https://en.wikipedia.org/wiki/Mart%C3%ADn_de_Azpilcueta. Last modified January 23, 2024; accessed October 15, 2025.

Massey, Cade, and Richard H. Thaler. "The Loser's Curse: Decision Making and Market Efficiency in the National Football League Draft." *Management Science* 59, no. 7 (July 2013): 1479–95.

Mauboussin, Michael J. *The Success Equation: Untangling Skill and Luck in Business, Sports, and Investing.* Harvard Business Review Press, 2012.

Mauboussin, Michael J., and Dan Callahan. "If You Can't Measure It, You Can't Manage It: Improving the Art and Science of Sell Decisions." *Credit Suisse Global Financial Strategies*, 2016.

Miller, Joshua B., and Adam Sanjurjo. "Surprised by the Hot Hand Fallacy? A Truth in the Law of Small Numbers." *Econometrica* 86, no. 6 (December 2018): 2019–47.

Munger, Charles T. *Poor Charlie's Almanack: The Wit and Wisdom of Charles T. Munger (Abridged).* Donning, 2005.

Nikolopoulou, Kassiani. "What Is Confirmation Bias? | Definition & Examples." *Scribbr.* September 19, 2022. https://qa.scribbr.co.uk/bias-in-research/confirmation-bias-explained/. Revised March 10, 2023. Accessed October 15, 2025.

Ovid. *Ars Amatoria.* Translated by J. H. Mozley. Loeb Classical Library. Harvard University Press, 1929.

Parrish, Shane. "Mental Models: The Best Way to Make Intelligent Decisions (~100 Models Explained)." *Farnam Street.* https://fs.blog/mental-models/. Accessed February 3, 2026.

Pink, Daniel H. *Drive: The Surprising Truth About What Motivates Us.* Riverhead, 2009.

Potter, Jaime. "The Ideal Team Size at Work May Be Smaller Than You Think." *Forbes*, April 27, 2020. https://www.forbes.com/sites/jaimepotter/2020/04/27/the-ideal-team-size-at-work-may-be-smaller-than-you-think. Accessed October 15, 2025.

Ptak, Jeffrey, Amy Arnott, Nikhil Chidurala, Michael Manetta, and Sandeep. *Mind the Gap US 2025.* Morningstar, 2025. https://www.morningstar.com/business/insights/research/mind-the-gap. Accessed February 3, 2025.

Randazzo, Anthony, and Jonathan Moody. "State of Pensions 2025." *Equable Institute.* https://equable.org/state-of-pensions-2025/. Accessed October 15, 2025.

Schwartz, Barry. *The Paradox of Choice: Why More Is Less.* HarperCollins, 2004.

Schwartz, Peter. *The Art of the Long View: Planning for the Future in an Uncertain World.* Currency/Doubleday, 1996.

Shefrin, Hersh, and Meir Statman. "The Disposition to Sell Winners Too Early and Ride Losers Too Long." *Journal of Finance* 40, no. 3 (1985): 777–90.

Shlaes, Amity. *Coolidge.* Harper, 2013.

Silver, Nate. "Final Election Update: There's a Wide Range of Outcomes, and Most of Them Come Up Clinton." *FiveThirtyEight*, November 8, 2016. https://fivethirtyeight.com/features/final-election-update-theres-a-wide-range-of-outcomes-and-most-of-them-come-up-clinton/. Accessed October 15, 2025.

Silver, Nate. *On the Edge: The Art of Risking Everything.* Penguin, 2024.
Sklansky, David. *The Theory of Poker: A Professional Poker Player Teaches You How to Think Like One.* Two Plus Two Publishing, 1999.
Spira, David. "Solve This Crossword in Less Than 12 Minutes and You Could Have Been a WWII Codebreaker." *Room Escape Artist.* February 11, 2017. https://roomescapeartist.com/2017/02/11/solve-this-crossword-in-less-than-12-minutes-and-you-could-have-been-a-wwii-codebreaker/. Accessed October 15, 2025.
Staw, Barry M. "Knee-Deep in the Big Muddy: A Study of Escalating Commitment to a Chosen Course of Action." Organizational Behavior and Human Performance 16, no. 1 (1976): 27–44.
"The Superinvestors of Graham-and-Doddsville." *Wikipedia: The Free Encyclopedia.* Last edited October 4, 2025. https://en.wikipedia.org/wiki/The_Superinvestors_of_Graham-and-Doddsville. Accessed October 15, 2025.
Surowiecki, James. *The Wisdom of Crowds.* Doubleday, 2004.
Svenson, Ola. "Are We All Less Risky and More Skillful Than Our Fellow Drivers?" *Acta Psychologica* 47, no. 2 (1981): 143–48.
Taleb, Nassim Nicholas. *The Black Swan: The Impact of the Highly Improbable.* Random House, 2007.
Tetlock, Philip E., and Dan Gardner. *Superforecasting: The Art and Science of Prediction.* Crown Publishers, 2015.
Thaler, Richard H. "Mental Accounting Matters." *Journal of Behavioral Decision Making* 12, no. 3 (September 1999): 183–206.
Thaler, Richard H. "Toward a Positive Theory of Consumer Choice." *Journal of Economic Behavior and Organization* 1, no. 1 (March 1980): 39–60.
Thaler, Richard H., and Cass R. Sunstein. *Nudge: Improving Decisions About Health, Wealth, and Happiness.* Yale University Press, 2008.
Tversky, Amos. "The Framing of Decisions and the Psychology of Choice." *Science* 211, no. 4481 (January 30, 1981): 453–58.
Tversky, Amos. "Prospect Theory: An Analysis of Decision Under Risk." *Econometrica* 47, no. 2 (March 1979): 263–91.
Tversky, Amos, and Daniel Kahneman. "Judgment Under Uncertainty: Heuristics and Biases." *Science* 185, no. 4157 (September 27, 1974): 1124–31.
Vaughan, Diane. *The Challenger Launch Decision: Risky Technology, Culture, and Deviance at NASA.* University of Chicago Press, 1996.
Viesturs, Ed, with David Roberts. *No Shortcuts to the Top: Climbing the World's Fourteen Highest Peaks.* Broadway, 2006.